THE LITTLE BOOK
OF BIG STUFF
ABOUT THE BRAIN

The true story of your amazing brain

THIS BOOK IS ABOUT YOUR BRAIN!

Written and illustrated by
Andrew Curran Edited by Ian Gilbert

Crown House Publishing Limited
www.crownhouse.co.uk
www.crownhousepublishing.com

First published by

Crown House Publishing Ltd
Crown Buildings, Bancyfelin, Carmarthen, Wales, SA33 5ND, UK
www.crownhouse.co.uk

and

Crown House Publishing Company LLC
6 Trowbridge Drive, Suite 5, Bethel, CT 06801, USA
www.Crownhousepublishing.com

First published 2008. Reprinted 2009, 2012.

British Library Cataloguing-in-Publication Data
A catalogue entry for this book is available
from the British Library.

Print ISBN 978-184590085-4
Mobi ISBN 978-184590276-6
ePub ISBN 978-184590209-4

LCCN 2007938976

Printed and bound in the UK by
Gomer Press, Llandysul, Ceredigion

To living,
the only real experience

Contents

Foreword

'To enhance public awareness of the benefits to be derived from brain research, the Congress, by House Joint Resolution 174, has designated the decade beginning January 1, 1990, as the "Decade of the Brain" and has authorized and requested the President to issue a proclamation in observance of this occasion.

Now, therefore, I, George Bush, President of the United States of America, do hereby proclaim the decade beginning January 1, 1990, as the Decade of the Brain. I call upon all public officials and the people of the United States to observe that decade with appropriate programs, ceremonies, and activities.

In Witness Whereof, I have hereunto set my hand this seventeenth day of July, in the year of our Lord nineteen hundred and ninety, and of the Independence of the United States of America the two hundred and fifteenth.'[1]

It was with these words that President George Bush opened the Decade of the Brain, a period of unprecedented collaboration, research and discovery focused on advancing our understanding of the human brain. (And it was these words, 'Mr Prime Minister. Thank you for being such a fine host for the OPEC summit' that President George W. Bush, thanked Australian Prime Minister John Howard at the opening of the APEC Summit in September 2007.)

---

1 Presidential Proclamation 6158

Since that time there have been many amazing discoveries concerning the grey matter between our ears, more so than at any other point in history. In fact, it is argued that 95% of what we know about the brain has been learned in the last 15 years or so. We have come a long way in the centuries since Aristotle was arguing that the heart was the centre of sensation and movement and even in the decades since Dr Walter J. Freeman was inserting an ice pick up through the eye socket of mentally ill patients to scrape away a bit of brain in his pioneering transorbital lobotomies.[2]

One of the key discoveries has been the extent to which we are able to 'grow our own brains'. That the actual physical architecture of our brains – the way our millions of brains cells are wired up together – is as a result of the experiences we have and have not had through our lives; nature and nurture working together to create something quite unique.

An example of the way our experiences mould our brains is found in research conducted on nine stringed instrument players and reported in *Science* magazine in 1995[3]. Experiments with these professional musicians showed how more of their brain was being used to process information coming from the fingers on their left hands than in non-musicians. They had changed the way their brain

---

2 *The Lobotomist*, El-Hai, Jack; John Wiley & Sons, New Jersey, 2005

3 Quoted in *Mind Sculpture*, Robertson, Ian; Transworld Publishers, London, 1999

was working by the repetitive experiences they had had. What's more, when the researchers probed further to see where the 'extra' brain had come from they were not entirely surprised to discover that it had been appropriated from the area of the brain normally associated with the palm of the left hand. What's more, it was ascertained that 'what determined how big the left-hand brain area had become was how old they were when they began to learn their instruments'.

The brain's ability to be moulded is known as 'plasticity' and the younger we are, the more plastic our brain is. That doesn't mean to say that you can't teach an old dog new tricks because you can (if the dog isn't too arrogant to think it knows it all and can't be bothered to change). It's just that it is harder to do, as you have to unwire certain patterns and rewire your brain with new pathways.

And this is one of the great uplifting themes running through this book: that by understanding how you have ended up with the brain you have both as a member of the human race and as an individual, you can actually come to love it better, understand it more and even know how to get more from it should you wish.

And this latter idea, that you can change your mind – literally – is another of the great breakthroughs in our understanding of one of the most remarkable outputs of the human brain – intelligence.

For a century the notion of intelligence has been linked to the idea of IQ. That you have an 'intelligence quotient' – your mental age divided by your chronological age multiplied by 100 and known as 'g' – that can be assessed, measured and recorded, that is fixed and God-given and by that you can know your station in life and your place in society. For a better understanding of the many flaws in the IQ-model of the world of human potential I recommend *The Making of Intelligence* by Ken Richardson from the Open University[4].

Richardson points out that this original equation was developed by a Frenchman, Francis Binet, at the turn of the last century as way of ascertaining which children needed the most amount of educational support at school. The educationally beneficial aspects of this process were overlooked, though, by people such as Lewis Terman in the US who pounced on Binet's work as a way of scientifically identifying 'feeblemindedness' in society in order to 'preserve our state for a class of people worthy to possess it'.[5]

One of the greatest ironies of modern psychology must be the fact that a series of IQ tests Terman performed on a particular class of young students failed to identify not one but two future Nobel laureates in physics, Luis Alvarez and William Shockley. (Indeed, Shockley's biographer describes his subject as 'the living embodiment of the weakness of IQ tests').[6]

---

4 *The Making of Intelligence*, Richardson, Ken; BCA, 1999
5 Quoted in ibid.
6 The rise and fall of William Shockley, *New Scientist*, 10 June 2006

Another American psychologist, Henry H. Goddard, also used the new Stanford-Binet IQ Test for socially manipulative purposes. With waves of new immigrants arriving in the US daily, Goddard pressed for IQ testing stations to be set up at their point of entry into the country. Here, using IQ tests delivered in English through interpreters, he was able to identify that '83% of Hungarians, 79% of Italians and 87% of Russians were feebleminded'[7].

What Richardson points out is the absurdly circular idea that the sorts of questions used in IQ tests were exactly the sorts of questions that children doing well at school would be able to answer. So, children doing well at school would do well in IQ tests and children who did well at IQ tests did well at school, thus proving how effective the IQ tests were.

As this book will show you – and as Dr Curran has pointed out elsewhere – there is a place for IQ testing but only as one element in a 'battery' of tests to help identify an individual's strengths and weaknesses. Add to this the idea of multiple intelligence (Professor Howard Gardner's theory that we don't just have one way of being 'clever' but at least eight and probably more[8]); the notion that we can teach people to be clever (see the work of Reuven Feuerstein based in Israel and known as 'instrumental enrichment'[9]) and our ability to 'grow' our brain and you

7 ibid.

8 *Frames of Mind: Theory of Multiple Intelligence*, Gardner, Howard; Basic Books, New York, 1983

9 *Changing Children's Minds: Feuerstein's Revolution in the Teaching of Intelligence*, Sharron, Howard; Souvenir Press, London, 1987

can begin to appreciate that the most staggering thing about our brain is not what it is but what it can become.

But, before you plunge into Dr Curran's story of how your brain became let me take you back to the Whitehouse one more time.

President Clinton (that's former US President Bill Clinton, not presidential candidate/failed presidential candidate/ President/Former President* Hilary Clinton) made himself a sticker for his fridge door during his campaign for re-election. It said, simply, 'It's the economy, stupid!' In other words, no matter how complicated and difficult things get, if he could remember to focus on this one thing alone then he would be OK.

In the work that I do with teachers around the world I urge them to do something similar for their staffroom doors, only this time the sticker should read, 'It's the brain, stupid!' Everything that goes on in classrooms, for better or for worse, is a result of activity between ears. And if you understand that, then no matter how complicated and difficult things get, you have a chance to do something about it.

And whatever role you have in life as you pick up this intriguing little book, the same rings true for you. Every act you undertake, every thought you entertain, every memory you hold, every hang up you have, every quirk,

---

* Delete as appropriate

foible, idiosyncrasy and knack, it's all the result of chemicals and electricity working across a network of soft organic matter that you have helped build throughout your life.

So, enjoy the story of your brain but remember, as someone once said, 'If our brains were simple enough to understand them, we would be too simple to understand them'.

Ian Gilbert
Suffolk
January 2008

Introduction

all it takes is love

This book is about the brain. I hope however it is mostly about who we all are, or at least how we arrived at being the person we are now. It is extraordinary to me how much understanding of myself and how much hope flows from my ongoing study of how the brain works. And perhaps the most surprising message for me from looking through billions of dollars of research is that the most important thing you can do for yourself and for others is to love yourself and others for who they are, because by doing that you maximise the brain's ability to learn and unlearn.

This book is about that understanding. It is a book about structure and function - and the immensely reassuring fact that there is nothing occult or sinister or hidden about our emotional selves - there is just a whole pile of circuitry that can be adjusted and changed and remodelled as required.

I like to take a simple approach to life and try to find easy ways to look at complex problems. And for us as humans our own brain is probably one of the most complex things we are ever going to encounter. So this book is about trying to make that unbelievably complex set of connections and interactions and cells and chemistry into something that can be understood at the most important level of all - as a human being alive with potential and ready to change in the pursuit of growth.

The work underlying the hypotheses and ideas in this book started with a neurosurgical friend of mine in England about 12 years ago, and since then I have been adding (and subtracting) thoughts and concepts until the present book distilled itself out of the process. I have to say it is a work in evolution - ideas that I present in this book may very well be proven incorrect as further work appears from the many laboratories and theorists around the world who are so heavily involved in trying to under-stand our brains (with their own brains, which is a fas-cinating thought - the brain is the only organ in the body which we study with itself!).

In defence of this book however I would say that as I continue to read deeply within the scientific literature, I have yet to find anything that disagrees with the funda-mental frameworks in this book. I am also encouraged by other sources of literature from outside hard–hatted sci-ence which also increasingly seem to support the most important message in this book - emotions and our emo-tional brains underpin everything we learn, and the more you have connected with another human being emotion-ally the more they can learn from you.

This is not a book about education in any narrow sense of that word. We are, in an absolutely fundamental way, an expression of how our brains are functioning. For every single one of us as human beings therefore to understand how our brains work means we have taken another step towards understanding ourselves. There is also a wonderful sense of hope for me in understanding how our brains work. That comes from the fact that there is nothing about ourselves that we can't fundamentally change if we are prepared to do the work required. This means that no matter how deep the damage runs, there is still hope that it can (eventually) be unlearned - or at least diluted to a level where it no longer governs our lives. It is extraordinary to consider that we are, in every aspect of our humanity, from how we brush our hair to the deepest of our religious convictions, just sets of circuits firing to produce reactions in our bodies and minds. I say 'just', but of course this isn't a 'just'; this is a dance of unsurpassing beauty that chimes with the music of the heavens.

Let me just share with you a small piece of synchronicity that occurred while I was working on one of the original draft papers that represented the earliest stage of the ideas in this book. For quite a long time when I was preparing the draft, the title read 'How the Brian works'. It took me several months to spot the error - Microsoft Word spell checker of course does not recognise that the name Brian is not grammatically particularly useful in this sentence! The synchronicity was down to the fact that I have always been a huge Monty Python fan. If the supposition of this book is correct - that we all are the sum total of our brain in what we express as humans - then the seat of godhood is indeed, as so many religions

3

believe, within each and every one of us, waiting to be found as we progress through life.

I would also like to say at this stage that the model of global brain functioning that I am describing in this book is to describe the vessel and not the spirit. I personally see the spirit as being separate from our human existence and do not attempt to try to understand something that I believe to be beyond the compass of the human mind. I would also say that this discussion is describing the anatomy and chemistry - that it is not in any way supposed to be a comment on all the functions of the brain.

That being said I hope that you really enjoy this book. It is supposed to be a relatively light-hearted look at brain functioning, though it is based firmly in the literature. As you will notice I have included a complete bibliography with this work and these papers and books would be available to everyone either through the Internet (where they will mostly be paid for) or through your local library.

Thank you for reading this.

Chapter 1

where it all came from

So how can I start to share with you the amazing science behind the theories about your brain and how it works so that you can hopefully understand yourself better? I love stories, and for me all good stories have a beginning, a middle and an end. I plan therefore to start the story of your brain right back at the first beginning we can really get any handle on - the beginning of life as we know it (Jim).

A really, really long time ago when the first land dwelling life was crawling on probably 17 wobbly legs out of the primeval swamp, your far distant ancestor probably looked extraordinarily ugly and had all the thinking ability of a rather unpleasant, two-month-old wet sponge. In fact, that very early ancestor was very probably not something you would have wanted to take home to meet your mother.

Nature is of course interested in change and growth (by and large). So after another really, really long time the wet sponge gradually grew a nervous system (you have to have a nervous system if you are going to do any of the most basic functions - such as moving, eating, having babies, etc.). That nervous system (through a process of incredibly complex evolution) ended up as the deepest and most primitive part of your brain, the so-called

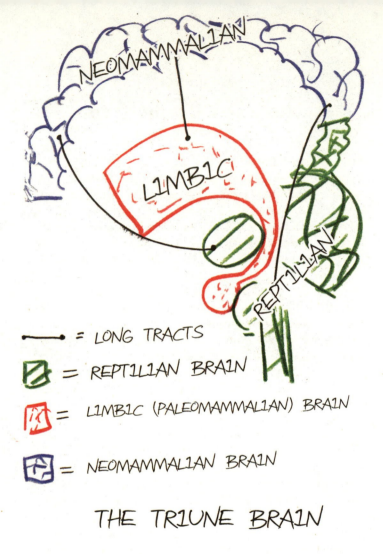

THE TR1UNE BRA1N

Figure 1

The deepest and most primitive part of your brain, the so-called *reptilian brain* (the green bit).

reptilian brain (the green bit in Figure 1). This was the first step towards evolving what P. D. MacLean[1] has called the triune brain, the ultimate expression of which is seen in you.

The reptilian brain is a pretty simple soul (Figure 2) and is pretty poor at responding to novel situations[2,3]. It represents the most basic form of complex higher nervous system evolution and had pride of place in the evolutionary tree about 400 million years ago. It sat in the heads of the immediate ancestor of the mammals (to which you of course belong), the birds, and those most ferocious of ferocious things, the dinosaurs (Figure 3). Its entire life aim was (and is) to preserve its own existence. It did this with little concern for any other life forms on the planet. This central need for self–preservation is of course a fundamental part of all our survival - the problem with lizards is that they do it as islands of individuality, not as functioning parts of a larger social group (which isn't a problem if you are a lizard, but is if you happen to be a human being!). And of course you still have a fully functioning, self–serving reptilian brain set deep into your brain.

It has a set of relatively primitive structures that are essential for the basic needs of being able to move, smell and see. It also carries the central structures that keep your heart beating and your lungs pumping - pretty important really for staying alive! It is these structures that are irreversibly damaged in the tragedy of 'brain stem death' - which I am sure you have heard about on

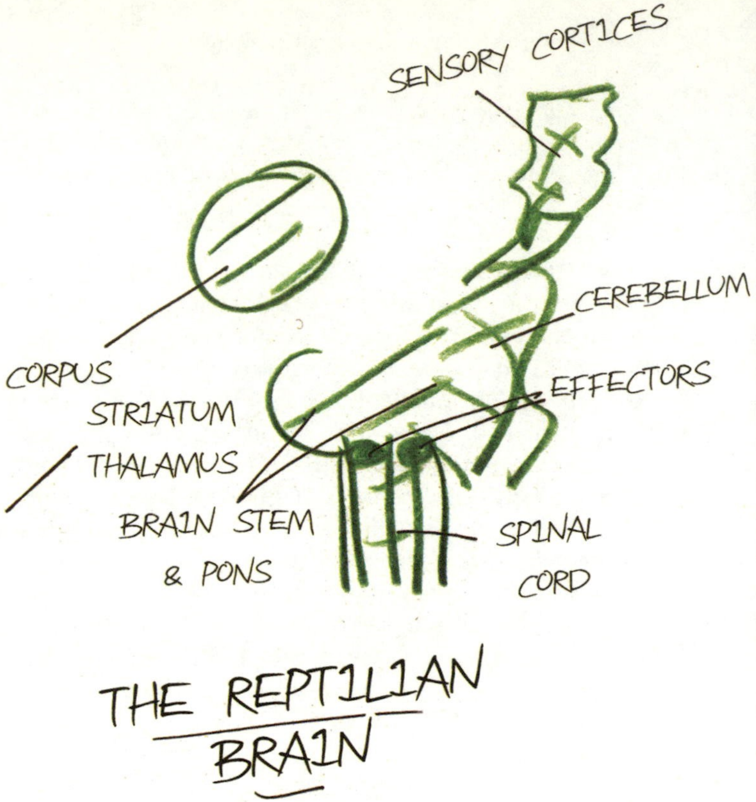

SENSORY CORTICES

CEREBELLUM

EFFECTORS

CORPUS
STRIATUM
THALAMUS
BRAIN STEM
& PONS

SPINAL
CORD

THE REPTILIAN
BRAIN

Figure 2

The reptilian brain is a pretty simple soul and is pretty poor at responding to novel situations.

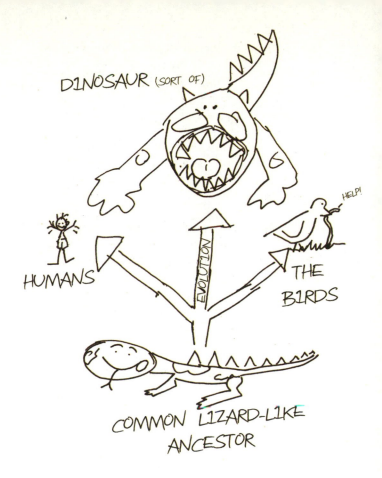

Figure 3

The reptilian brain sat in the heads of the immediate ancestor of the mammals, the birds, and those most ferocious of ferocious things, the dinosaurs.

television and in films, if not in your own life. Finally, it has a primitive form of what in you has become your *amyg–dala*. This very early and primitive emotional structure is to do with what are called 'flight or fight' reactions, i.e. either run from whatever is threatening you - or hit it[4;5]! The amygdala (of which I am going to tell you a great deal more later) also carries the centre(s) for sexual arousal.

Outside these essential but ultimately basic functions the reptilian brain's ability to perform more complex tasks is extremely limited. In fact it is estimated that in its most highly evolved state (and the well reported example of this highly evolved state is the Mexican green lizard) this brain is capable of 27 different behaviours. These behaviours (whilst they might tax the brain of my uncle Thomas at three in the morning after a good Friday night feed of drink) are not complex and involve things like moving from the heat to the shade, from the shade to the heat, and finding water. The most complex behaviours that reptiles get up to are to do with active and passive stances (Figure 4)[3]. These are slightly more complex and involve a small lizard crouching down submissively when confronted by a large lizard, and the larger lizard standing up aggressively. This stops the larger lizard from attacking the smaller lizard and therefore wins as a top–notch survival behaviour. In human behaviour the very same thing still goes on - after all in every corridor of power exactly the same survival behaviours can be witnessed!

BIG LIZARD BEING AS BIG AS POSSIBLE

LITTLE LIZARD TRYING TO BE AS FLAT AS POSSIBLE

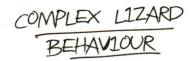

COMPLEX LIZARD BEHAVIOUR

Figure 4

The most complex behaviours that reptiles get up to are to do with active and passive stances.

Its desire for survival makes the reptilian brain egocentric, self-serving and appetite-driven, and it is almost certainly without a conscience of any sort. In terms of our own evolutionary tree this brain had probably reached the peak of its development about 250 million years ago, perhaps longer. As I have said from this brain the birds, the dinosaurs and we humans developed. To turn into the sort of brain a bird or a dinosaur or a mammal could use the higher parts of the reptilian brain grew in different directions. In mammals there was increasing attention to smell as a major sense and then finally the development of a complex *cortex* (that's the main bit of our brain that you can see when you look at a human brain - it's all covered in lumps and bumps and looks like a huge walnut), which of course is what finally differentiates ourselves and other primates from the rest of mammals.

Birds of course grew a birdbrain (!) and as for the dinosaurs we don't know what their brains looked like. As all we have ever found are just the empty skulls of dinosaurs it is almost impossible to know what the structure of the dinosaur brain was from these. It is interesting to see that there is an increasing thought (as portrayed so lovingly in the *Jurassic Park* films) that dinosaurs may have been nurturing creatures - though for smaller creatures to be part of the nurturing process for Tyrannosaurus rex must have been a very short and extremely painful experience! This concept of the dinosaurs as nurturing, if it is correct, suggests that at least in part their brains may have developed along similar lines to our own - nurturing requires a very specialist part of the brain as I will discuss next.

The next step in the evolutionary process was to attach higher brain to the reptilian foundation. In the case of mammals this seems predominantly to have been the *limbic* or emotional brain (also called the paleomammalian brain) (Figure 5)[6]. The effect of this was to transform our rather repellent self–centred reptiles into increasingly social animals who nurtured their young and lived together in communities[2;7]. Not that these early mammals set up a National Health Service designed for the egocentrically challenged but they did increasingly seem to function as co–operating individuals rather than islands in a tempestuous life. In you this part of the brain is huge and occupies a great deal of your higher cortex. In fact it has been argued that an entire layer of our cortices is given over to the limbic system.

At this stage we enter a rather chicken and egg argument. Did the development of these new higher brain centres drive social and nurturing behaviours to develop or did these behaviours drive the development of the higher brain? This question is ultimately unanswerable as any individual must be a result of nurture's interaction with nature. For me I do feel that the development of higher centres came first, bringing with them extra nerve cells. These extra nerve cells (or *neurones*) would have increased the brain's ability to perform new functions. Later on I will discuss in more detail why this should be but for the moment you can just take my word for it - the more nerve cells you have the more ability you have for complex behaviours (Figure 6).

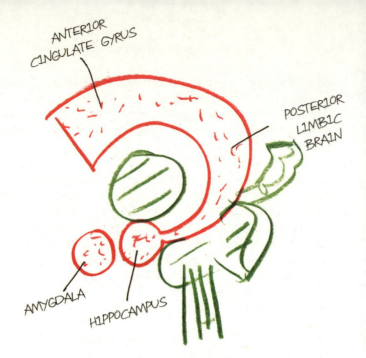

ANTERIOR CINGULATE GYRUS

POSTERIOR LIMBIC BRAIN

AMYGDALA

HIPPOCAMPUS

▤ = REPTILIAN BRAIN

▨ = PALEOMAMMALIAN (LIMBIC) BRAIN

NON-PRIMATE MAMMALIAN BRAIN

Figure 5

The next step in the evolutionary process was to attach higher brain to the reptilian foundation. In the case of mammals this seems predominantly to have been the *limbic* or emotional brain (also called the paleomammalian brain).

With all these extra neurones the development of these new functions may have led to increased co-operation between individuals and this then improved survival. And of course if you are surviving better you are breeding more and your offspring will carry these characteristics with them. So the early mammals, in my opinion, would have had to develop extra brain cells first and then any behaviours occurring by chance which were successful, that is to say resulted in the survival and successful breeding of that individual, may have dynamically direct-ed the way in which the new brain specialised. If that all sounds rather complicated please stick with the thought that nerve cells equal behaviours - and the more nerve cells you have the more complex your behaviour can be. There is also an extraordinary beauty in the thought that it all just happens - behaviours have the ability to create brain specialisation and this ability is still intrinsic in how our own human brains develop.

But to get back to the story about why your brain looks the way it does, I have now reached a stage in the story of our evolution where your brain has developed a paleo-mammallian, emotional brain wrapped around a deep reptilian core designed for your survival against all odds. This core has been integrated with the new higher limbic or paleomammalian brain. This part of your brain is con-cerned with more complex behaviours such as interacting with other members of the same species and caring for the young. Nature is very sensible, and the newer, more complex limbic brain didn't take over functions from the reptilian brain, but instead added functions of its own,

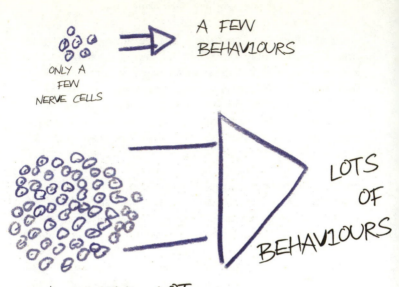

ONLY A FEW NERVE CELLS

A FEW BEHAVIOURS

AN AWFUL LOT OF NERVE CELLS

LOTS OF BEHAVIOURS

BEHAVIOURS INCREASE WITH INCREASING NUMBERS OF NERVE CELLS

Figure 6
The more nerve cells you have the more ability you have for complex behaviours.

using the basic survival functions in the reptilian brain just as they were. The difference was that now these basic mechanisms were directed not only towards survival (obviously still of central importance) but also towards nurturing and social behaviours. After all, to do these behaviours you still use the same muscles, and these continue to require direct input from your reptilian brain to work.

So what happened next? The limbic brain probably first developed about 150 million years ago and for millions of years there doesn't seem to have been any other dramatic development. Then, quite suddenly, about four million years ago our immediate ancestors finally stood up in the savannah in Africa (Figure 7). These were little guys and dolls probably only about two feet tall and they seemed to have lived a simple and probably mostly nomadic existence across the plains of Africa. I think that it's likely that given their small size and the very large predators hanging around the savannah at the time, our earliest ancestors were mostly hunted rather than being hunters. My guess is they were very good at two things - hiding very well and running very fast!

These very early ancestors of ours had developed a new higher centre in their brains (Figure 8)[8]. This was so much bigger than the two previous parts of the brain that eventually it completely enfolded them in its embrace; in your brain all you can see on the outside is this new addition to the previous brain called the neomammalian brain. The increase in the number of nerve cells that the

AUSTRALOPITHECINE PERSON

Figure 7

About four million years ago our immediate ancestors finally stood up in the savannah in Africa.

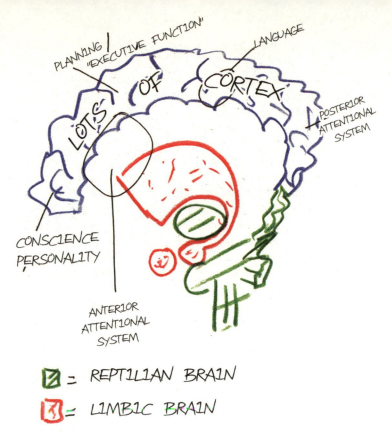

PLANNING / "EXECUTIVE FUNCTION"

LANGUAGE

OF CORTEX

LOTS

POSTERIOR ATTENTIONAL SYSTEM

CONSCIENCE PERSONALITY

ANTERIOR ATTENTIONAL SYSTEM

▨ = REPTILIAN BRAIN

▨ = LIMBIC BRAIN

▨ = NEOMAMMALIAN BRAIN

THE TRIUNE BRAIN WITH DETAILS OF NEOMAMMALIAN FUNCTIONS

Figure 8

These very early ancestors of ours had developed a new higher centre in their brains.

new neomammalian brain brought with it was stupendous (Figure 9). Whilst completely accurate numbers are not really known the reptilian brain probably has 15 to 20 million nerve cells, the limbic brain in the region of 100 million nerve cells and the present best guess for the number of nerve cells in a developed human brain is probably in the region of 150 billion. (This is your brain I am talking about. Reach up and feel your skull - in there is your brain - and that brain has 150 billion nerve cells in it! How extraordinary is that!) These numbers also throw into relief the massive steps forward that evolution took in increasingly shorter periods of time. The reptilian brain took probably two and a half billion years to reach its maximum development, the limbic brain took a further 200 million years and the new massive increase in cortex only took four million years! I find that absolutely extraordinary! Each step, despite meaning a massive increase in the number of neurones, took a shorter and shorter time to develop.

So now my story has reached what your brain is now: a deep lying, primitive reptilian brain, a much more complex emotional limbic brain and now this extraordinarily complex *neocortex* (meaning, very simply, 'new cortex') all working together as an integrated whole (Figure 1). So what difference did this massive increase in nerve cells make? The answer is that once again it increased the number of complex behaviours that our early ancestors and finally ourselves could perform (remember, the more nerve cells you have the more complex your behaviours can be).

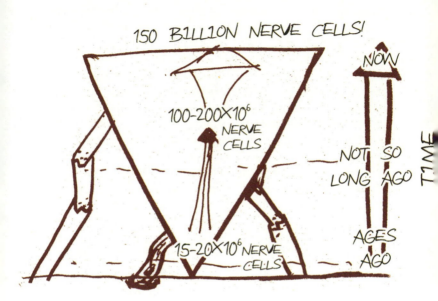

AN IRISH* PYRAMID DEMONSTRATING THE MASSIVE INCREASE IN NERVE CELLS.

* I'M IRISH. I SHOULD KNOW

Figure 9

The increase in the number of nerve cells that the new neomammalian brain brought with it was stupendous.

I mentioned earlier that the reptilian brain is capable of 27 different complex behaviours, and mammals are obviously capable of probably a hundred. Our brains however are capable of thousands of complex behaviours. Among these behaviours is the almost certainly unique human ability to be able to turn our thoughts inwards and observe ourselves and our own mental life. This is an extraordinarily powerful observation because it is only through this ability that you can understand your own emotions and hence the emotions of others. This is the central part to a great many of the techniques used in emotional healing. To quote P. D. MacLean, this evolutionary development made possible *'the insight required for the foresight to plan for the needs of others as well as the self - to use our knowledge to alleviate suffering everywhere'*[2].

And this gives the first inkling of how understanding brain function and structure can help us with healing ourselves from emotional damage. Evolution has provided you with a tool to untie your own and others' emotional knots. But to make further sense of that I want to explain how those knots got tied in the first place, and what 'tying an emotional knot' means at a structural level in your brain. I will deal with that whole concept later on. First let me finish the present discussion.

This ability to look inwards on your own thoughts is 'thinking about thinking' or *metacognition*, and we humans are probably unique in the living world in being able to do this. For the first time in evolutionary history your brain was consistently capable of introspection and all the unbelievably complex higher-level functioning that we take for granted. It is almost certainly these higher functions that made us first start to use tools and to develop a sense of past and future, which even the closest primates seem to have in only the most primitive forms.

So that is the story of how you ended up as the proud owner of the brain that you have within your skull. Understanding how these three different evolutionary parts of the brain work together is the job of the rest of this book. It is through understanding this that you can start to answer the questions that all this raises about emotional health. I believe that if we can understand the processes within the brain by which damage occurs, then all of us may be better equipped to heal that damage.

The first thing I want to do towards this deeper understanding of how your brain works is to answer the question that I have already brought up several times - why does increasing number of nerve cells equal increasingly complex behaviour? In the next chapter I will start to take this apart as we meet for the first time the concept of *templates* and *neural patterns*.

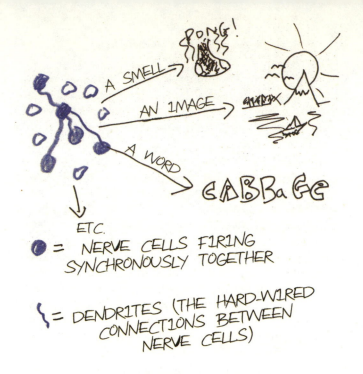

A SMELL →

AN IMAGE →

A WORD → CABBAGE

ETC.

● = NERVE CELLS FIRING SYNCHRONOUSLY TOGETHER

ʃ = DENDRITES (THE HARD-WIRED CONNECTIONS BETWEEN NERVE CELLS)

NOTE - A TEMPLATE PROBABLY USED HUNDREDS OF THOUSANDS OF NERVE CELLS

TEMPLATES

Figure 10

Something you remember might be a smell, a dream, a painful memory, a damaging remark, or simply making a movement, but it is because you have fired off a template (or a number of templates) that you remember it at all.

Chapter 2

a first look at the wiring

So, in your head is this amazing three-part, or 'triune' brain. Sitting on top of your spinal cord is the most primitive part, the reptilian brain driven by self-seeking, survival-based motivations. Its job is to keep you alive and reproducing irrespective of any other priority. Sitting just above it is your emotional brain, your limbic or paleomammalian brain concerned with nurturing, social functioning and all the complex behaviours that make that possible. And wrapped around them both is your huge neomammalian cortex, the repository of all your dreams made manifest and as full of ideas and thoughts as the heaven is of stars.

But how does it all work? How can you be sitting there and reading this book and the words make sense? How do you know that in a few minutes you will put the book down and go out for a pint with your friends? How can we humans have designed and made telephones or computers or even a good paring knife? And what happens when it all goes wrong? What is going on structurally in our brains that interferes with our emotional - and physical - health?

Templates. The answer is templates (Figure 10).[9;10, 11-16] So what on earth is a template when one is talking about the brain? The beginning of this part of the story started some 30 or 40 years ago when a very smart chap called Donald Hebb argued that you learn things because your nerve cells join together in a way that makes them fire together. He said that 'nerve cells that fire together wire together'. What is also now known is that this wiring together of nerve cells is predominantly under the control of your emotional system[17-19] - the more emotion in a situation the more likely it is you will learn from it. So here is the second piece of understanding about brain functioning in health and 'unhealth' - the wiring to–gether of nerve cells is predominantly under the control of your emotional system. This means that your emotional self is centrally involved in creating who you are. Not very surprising, but very interesting that this is a central fact of brain structure and function. I will be talking a lot more about this later.

For now, I want you to think a little more about templates, these wired–together nerve cells that form patterns. When a nerve template fires you remember something because everything in your brain is stored in the form of these templates[9;20-22]. That something you remember might be a smell, a dream, a painful memory, a damaging remark, or simply making a movement, but it is because you have fired off a template (or a number of templates) that you remember it at all (Figure 10). Nerve cells that have formed connections with each other do so in a very specific manner. They actually grow long, incredibly thin projections out from their cell walls looking for other nerve cells that are firing at the same time as them. I find that truly wonderful - they actually go out looking for partners that are completely in tune with them! Once they find a partner nerve cell, they form a *synapse* with them (Figure 11). A synapse is how two nerve cells communicate with each other. Incredibly, they don't actually touch. Instead they leave a very tiny gap between the two ends of their connection so that chemicals can move back and forth across the gap between them - and these chemicals miraculously carry messages between the two nerve cells (Figure 11).

Because the communication is by chemicals, it is theoretically possible to administer a neurochemical called *acetylcholine* into the brain, and if the dose was of exactly the right concentration throughout the brain, it would switch off all the connections between your nerve cells[23-25]. If the nerve cell connections had been turned off in this manner in your brain so that none of your templates worked, you would then become like a newborn infant without memories or behaviours except at the most primitive level. In fact you would have been 'brain washed'.

Templates are of course something that you are already familiar with. The simplest example of a template would be cutting a shape from cardboard so that you could trace around it to accurately replicate it on a piece of paper (Figure 12). The piece of cardboard that you trace round is the template. If you keep that piece of cardboard safely you can use it again and again to produce exactly the same shape from other pieces of cardboard. In your brain a template is the pattern that a group of nerve cells that

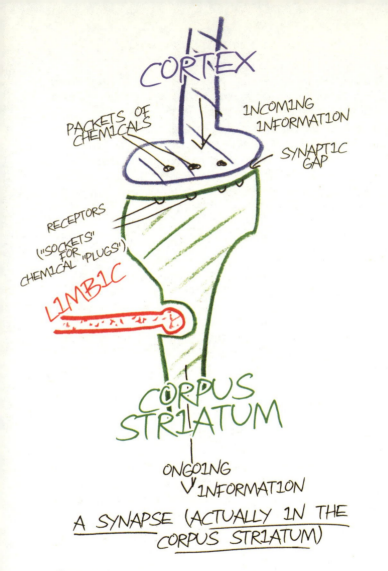

Figure 11

Chemicals miraculously carry messages between the two nerve cells.

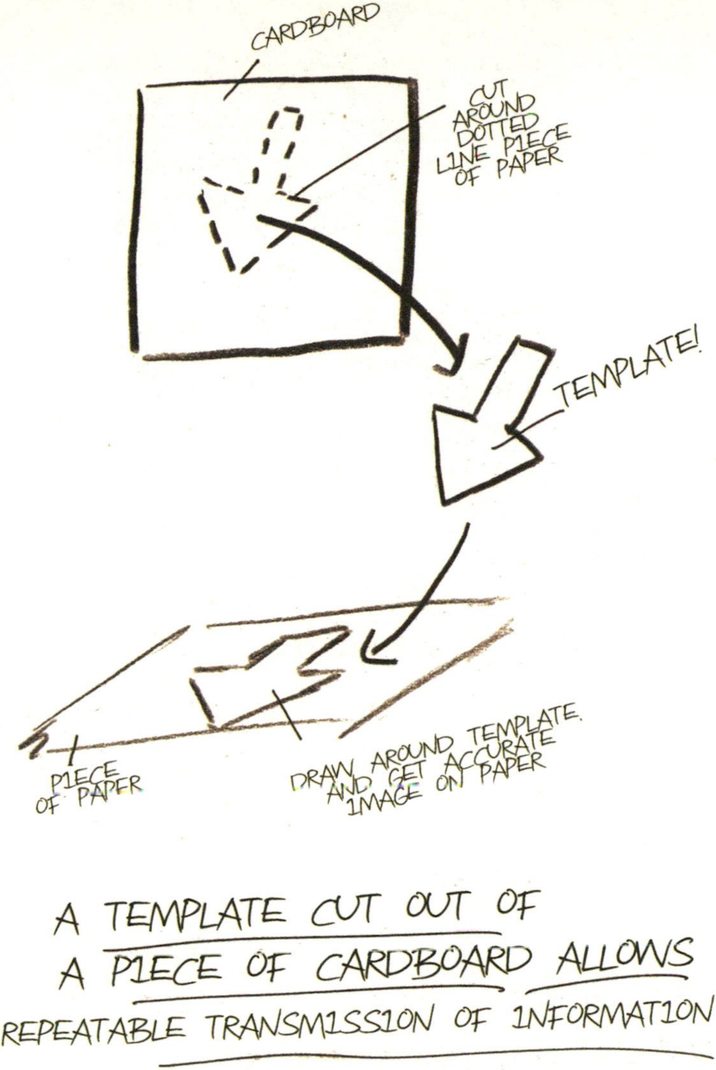

CARDBOARD

CUT AROUND DOTTED LINE PIECE OF PAPER

TEMPLATE!

PIECE OF PAPER

DRAW AROUND TEMPLATE, AND GET ACCURATE IMAGE ON PAPER

A TEMPLATE CUT OUT OF A PIECE OF CARDBOARD ALLOWS REPEATABLE TRANSMISSION OF INFORMATION

Figure 12

The simplest example of a template would be cutting a shape from cardboard so that you could trace around it to accurately replicate it on a piece of paper.

have been connected together make. This template (and all the other millions of templates you have in your head) represents a piece of information. That piece of information may be a word or a smell or part of a movement, indeed anything that your brain does.

So you have all your data, your memories stored as templates. But how does your brain use these templates to function? For there is no doubt that we do function, though a lot of that functioning may be dysfunctional.

To give you an example of how your brain uses templates I would like you to imagine that it is an extremely hot day in August. You have been out for a good bit of retail therapy with your partner and your three children aged nearly 7, 5 and 3 (Figure 13). As you are a very dedicated retail therapist you started at the huge mall near your house at 8.30 in the morning. It is now 6.30 in the evening and you are standing outside the door of a large department store and in your hands are copious shopping bags. Your 7-year-old spotted a toy that he wanted three and a half hours ago in some sort of gadget shop and is still explaining to you why this toy would be so important to him. Each explanation lasts 30 seconds and he is repeating these at exactly two minute intervals. Your 5-year-old has just vomited up the hotdog that she ate two hours ago and is playing with the result on the floor of the mall, and your 3-year-old has just wet his pants. Your partner disappeared at lunchtime 'to check the water in the car' and has not yet returned!

Figure 13

An extremely hot day in August. You have been out for a good bit of retail therapy.

Suffice to say that you have had enough. Your emotional system is saying 'GO HOME. GO HOME. GO HOME!' However you have a problem. For you to get from outside the department store to get home you need to form a plan, otherwise you will still be standing there with your shopping and your kids when the security men come round. 'Plans' in the sense I am talking about are how your higher, more complex brain areas function. They pull together bits of information and combine them together to create an action 'plan'. It is this concept of creating a plan of action that I want to unpack for you now.

So what do you need to make your plan? Well, as an example of some of the information you will need for this plan I would like you to imagine that your car is a dung beetle blue Ford Mondeo estate (Ford describes this colour as 'aquamarine mist' but it is exactly the same colour as an African dung beetle - you know, the ones that walk around backwards rolling a huge ball of dung with their back feet. Which, if you think about it is an almost perfect approach to life. After all, when asked what the smell is coming from your direction, you can reply: 'Smell? What smell?').

Your Ford Mondeo estate is parked in all its dung beetle blue elegance in one of the vast car parking areas beside the mall among thousands of other cars some of which are identical to yours. I want you to imagine that four parts of the plan that you need to get home are specific details about your car - for the obvious reason that if you can identify your car among all the others you can get into it and go home - and that is such a wonderful thought at this moment in time it makes you feel weak at the knees!

In Figure 14 I have drawn four groups of neurones. These are in specific parts of your brain. Group A is in your *corpus striatum*, an area of the brain that is probably to do with categorical memory, i.e. it stores templates in terms of categories. This is part of your reptilian brain (though in your brain it has become much more complex than what a Mexican green lizard carries around in its flat little skull) and is where the lizard (and you as well) store behavioural (or 'habitual') templates.

It seems likely that it is your emotional/limbic brain that can activate exactly the templates you need to create your plan (I'll talk more about this in a moment). The template that your limbic system has activated in your corpus striatum in this case is 'car'. If you look back to Figure 14 again, the Group B nerve cells are in your visual association cortex and in this case we will say that they store the pattern for 'estate'. Group C is also your visual association cortex and stores the pattern for the 'dung beetle blue'. To complete the identifiers of your particular dung beetle blue Ford Mondeo I have depicted a group of nerve cells (Group D) in the limbic or emotional cortex. This represents a rather more complex pattern. This particular template represents a unique identifying feature of your Ford Mondeo estate (because dung beetle blue, estate and the fact that your car is a Ford Mondeo are not going to be unique identifiers in a car park full of thousands of cars).

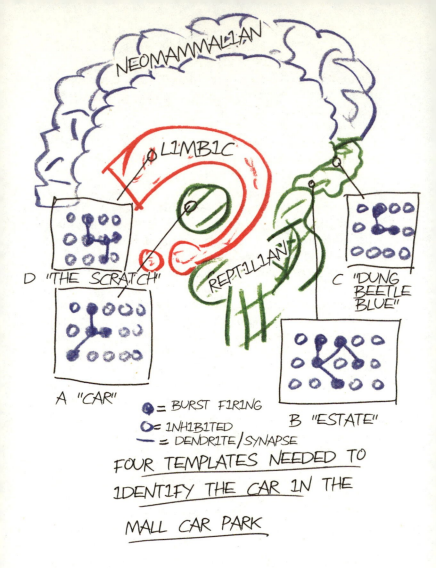

FOUR TEMPLATES NEEDED TO
IDENTIFY THE CAR IN THE
MALL CAR PARK

Figure 14

The four groups of neurones are in specific parts of your brain.

Little Johnny (the child at your feet who is STILL going on about the thing in the gadget shop) was given a chrome scooter for his fifth birthday one and a half years ago. Your then brand-new Ford estate was parked on your gently sloping drive when Johnny came out of the garage on his scooter and started down the same slow and gentle slope.

As he passed the front of your Ford estate the front wheel of his scooter bumped on a small pebble. This started a speed wobble that was heart-stoppingly alarming for young Johnny. With great good fortune however the handlebar of his chrome scooter landed on the very front of the passenger side of your brand new Ford Mondeo estate. Delighted that this had prevented him falling he continued on his way down the drive with the handlebar leaning against the side of the car as he proceeded rapidly towards the road. The resultant 15 foot long scratch is now a deep brown with the paint flaking off the rust as it eats its way into the metalwork. This emotional memory still has such strong ties in your brain that you get palpitations just thinking about it.

So now you have four separate items of information about your car which will enable you to find it in the mall car park - it is a dung beetle blue Ford Mondeo estate with a very long scratch down one side (there go those palpitations again!). These separate neuronal templates are however no good to you unless you can do two things. Firstly you need to bring them up to a functioning level of activation. What on earth does this mean? Well,

I want you to imagine that your brain and all its nerve cells are like a huge orchestra. Each nerve cell has an instrument and each nerve cell is a virtuoso performer. When they are all sitting waiting for the conductor, they are doing things independently of each other. One of the tuba players might be tuning his tuba. The third horn is talking on her mobile. The violinists are all independently putting on their makeup. And so on. There is no sense of order, things are just happening randomly and, most importantly, asynchronously (Figure 15).

Your brain in the resting state is exactly like this. It is ticking over at eight to 18 Hz ('Hz' means cycles per second) and your nerve cells are just bumbling along perfectly content in their own space. There is no synchronous activity.

Now I want you to imagine that the conductor has arrived and has taken her place at the front of the orchestra. Quite quickly the various independent activities stop and there is a sense of increasing synchrony in the actions of the musicians as they prepare to play the piece. In your own brain the conductor is predominantly the limbic, emotional brain. It is able to bring your nerve cells to attention (just as the conductor has done with the musicians) and then bring the nerve cells it wants to fire 'up to speed'. What does 'up to speed' mean to the brain? Well, this is perhaps one of the most wonderful, extraordinary things about how the brain works, and why the analogy with an orchestra is so apt. The functioning brain, your brain, actually produces harmonies within

A| 8-18H, ASYNCHRONOUS

B| > 20H, SYNCHRONOUS
(GAMMA RANGE)

A - RESTING STATE NERVE CELLS

B - NERVE CELLS "DOING WORK"

Figure 15

In A there is no sense of order, things are just happening randomly and, most importantly, asynchronously.

In B the rate of firing of the nerve cells is increased to a special rate known as the 'gamma rate.

itself, harmonies of nerve cell firing that underlie all your brain functions.

Let me unpack that for you in some detail. To make things happen in your brain, i.e. to get templates to activate and provide your brain with the information it needs to do anything, you have to increase the rate of firing of those nerve cells to a special rate known as the 'gamma rate' (Figure 15) (this is 20–500 Hz - which in itself is extraordinary; 500 cycles per second is really going for it!)[11–13;16;26–28]. But what is even more extraordinary is that these nerve cells don't just increase their firing rate, but they seem to do so synchronously and *in harmonic resonance* with the other nerve cells throughout the brain that are going to be involved in the plan you are preparing.

That is truly wonderful! Your brain works (predominantly) because your emotional system essentially selects *exactly* the nerve cells it needs from the 150 billion you have in your brain, brings them up to these extraordinary levels of firing (the gamma rate, 20–500 Hz) and does so synchronously and in harmonic resonance with each other. Now if that isn't a celestial orchestra, I don't know what is. It is literally mind–blowingly beautiful. Wow! It is not really known how this happens in detail but it is possible that your limbic system is able to stimulate a structure in your brain stem called the PPN (Figure 16) (*pedunculo–pontine nucleus* - about which you need know nothing more!) to release a special neurochemical called acetylcholine onto the nerve cells that you wish to use in

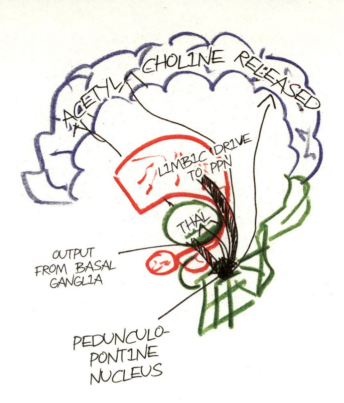

ACETYL CHOLINE RELEASED

LIMBIC DRIVE TO PPN

THAL

OUTPUT FROM BASAL GANGLIA

PEDUNCULO-PONTINE NUCLEUS

THAL = THALANMUS

THE PEDUNCULO-PONTINE NUCLEUS

Figure 16

It is possible that your limbic system is able to stimulate a structure in your brain stem called the PPN.

your template. Acetylcholine used in this way may facilitate the increasing level of excitation of the nerve cells so that they can readily reach the gamma rate. If this is the case then your limbic brain must be able to store patterns of activation within itself that can in turn accurately target the release of acetylcholine onto the nerve cells that you want for that particular plan. In this model the emotional brain is therefore the conductor - and the composer!

So lets get back to standing outside that department store with the kids and your shopping - AND NO !!!??$££ PARTNER! In your brain the four templates ('car', 'estate', 'dung beetle blue' and 'THE SCRATCH') are now firing at the gamma rate (Figure 17). However there is still a problem. You see, the templates are all in different parts of your brain, and none of these are conscious brain - so they can fire away all they want to but you will 'know' nothing about them. (By 'know' I mean you will not be conscious that they are firing). So your brain has to get these patterns somewhere where they can all be together at the same time (so you can make them into a plan) and where you can be consciously aware of the information they contain.

Well, your brain has a very specialised area of the neo-mammalian cortex called the *dorso–lateral prefrontal cortex* (or DLPFC which is easier to remember!) (Figure 18)[29;30] that serves exactly this purpose. Information in the form of templates can be uploaded into it from all over the brain, and if the bits of information arrive synchronously

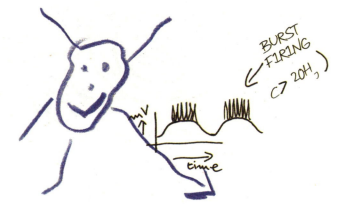

A NERVE CELL BURST
FIRING

Figure 17

In your brain the four templates are now firing at the gamma rate.

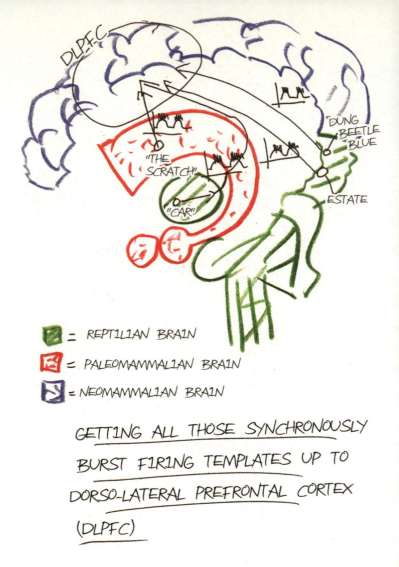

= REPTILIAN BRAIN

= PALEOMAMMALIAN BRAIN

= NEOMAMMALIAN BRAIN

GETTING ALL THOSE SYNCHRONOUSLY BURST FIRING TEMPLATES UP TO DORSO-LATERAL PREFRONTAL CORTEX (DLPFC)

Figure 18

The brain has a very specialised area of the neomammalian cortex called the dorso-lateral prefrontal cortex (DLPFC).

and in harmonic resonance with each other, you can use them to make a plan (or think about thinking, or have a dream, or anything really)[29;30]. It is probably fairly similar to RAM in a computer in that the 'programs' in the 'hard drives' of the rest of your brain produce the information which is then temporarily used in DLPFC before being dumped again to allow new information to be used. Unlike RAM however it almost certainly stores templates of its own and therefore can actively participate in the processes going on in it[31-33].

So let us now imagine that your four templates of 'car', 'estate', 'dung beetle blue', and 'THE SCRATCH' are transmitted to arrive in the DLPFC simultaneously, and probably in harmonic resonance with each other. This to me is a very beautiful thought - these harmonic resonances seem to be the same harmonics that we use in music and may underlie our enjoyment and need for music. It's like there's a full orchestra playing in our brains all the time, and what's even more wonderful is that in a healthy brain they play beautifully in tune. And if the main conductor is your emotional brain, then the healthier your emotional self, the more beautifully the orchestra will play.

So your DLPFC now has all the data points that it needs to begin making a plan. You have remembered that you have a dung beetle blue Ford Mondeo estate with a big scratch down one side. You do need other bits of information however. A very specialist structure called the *hippocampus* (Figure 19) adds pieces of information from what is called 'short term memory' about where you

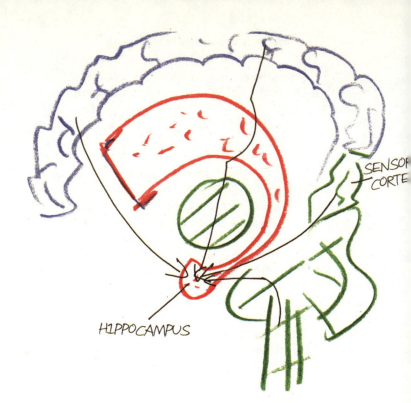

SENSOR
CORTE

HIPPOCAMPUS

THE HIPPOCAMPUS RECEIVES

INFORMATION INFLOW FROM

VIRTUALLY THE ENTIRE BRAIN

Figure 19

A very specialist structure called the *hippocampus* adds pieces of
information from what is called 'short term memory'.

parked the car and how to get there (I will talk a lot more about the hippocampus in the chapter on learning and memory).

Now with all the relevant information to make your plan, all you have to do is fire a specialist command template to the part of your brain that makes your body move, your *primary motor cortex* (Figure 20). This sends templates down to instruct your brain stem to start walking and off you go with your shopping and your children in tow.

To think a little about these specialist templates, called *command templates*, consider that they are probably how higher centres such as your DLPFC and your limbic brain send instructions to specialised areas further down the command chain (Figure 20). These command templates could be imagined to be like macros in a computer program. I know this can sound a bit daunting, but let me unpack it for you. A macro is actually a very simple thing. It is a single command that starts off a whole set of other commands to perform multiple functions. Imagine this is an army we are talking about. The general can't very well tell every single soldier under his or her command what to do individually. Instead, he or she will give an order to someone more junior than him (for example: Tell that goldarned fool on Bunker Hill to move platoon 4 across to the river and tell that other moron on Bottom Gully to move platoons 3 and 2 across to Bunker Hill. Oh, and while you're at it, tell those dratted fly boys to drop a lot of explosives just over the ridge at 03.20 hours on

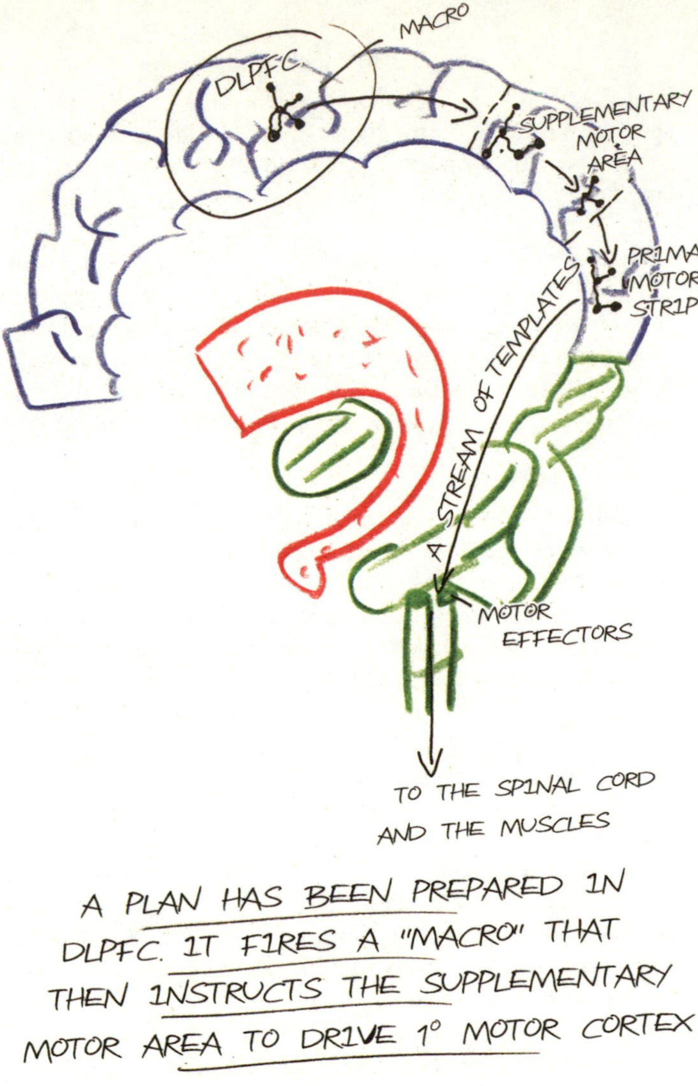
MACRO
DLPFC
SUPPLEMENTARY MOTOR AREA
PRIMARY MOTOR STRIP
A STREAM OF TEMPLATES
MOTOR EFFECTORS
TO THE SPINAL CORD AND THE MUSCLES
A PLAN HAS BEEN PREPARED IN DLPFC. IT FIRES A "MACRO" THAT THEN INSTRUCTS THE SUPPLEMENTARY MOTOR AREA TO DRIVE 1° MOTOR CORTEX

Figure 20

The DLPFC and your limbic brain send instructions to specialised areas further down the command chain.

coordinates Z233 Y54. The junior officer picks up the radio and passes each command on to the relevant soldier (or fly boy). They then pass the command on to all the men and women under their command - and so on. So one person (the general) with a couple of simple commands is able to get in motion hundreds or perhaps thousands of soldiers, each one of which can perform independent functions. The initial commands therefore are macros, triggering a chain reaction of events which become increasingly complex.

When we apply this to your brain, where a single command template from, for example a part of your higher cortex like the supplementary motor area (where you do your planning for movements and store templates to do with initiating movements), is capable of triggering a chain of templates from your primary motor cortex (which sits just beside it in your brain). This chain of templates is then streamed down to your brain stem (where you have all the necessary relay stations to convert the commands into signals that the spinal cord can understand) and contains all the information required to guide your muscles through the appropriate actions that they have been asked to do. Once the brain stem relays are activated, the signals pass on down the spinal cord where they activate the nerve cells that make your muscles work. And eureka, you start walking!

So once you have fired the command template(s), now you can finally get from outside the major department store to your car where you put the key in the lock and open the car, distribute the children in their various seats and sit yourself down in the seat behind the steering wheel. What a relief! The first thing that hits you (other than the 3-year-old's used ice lolly stick - with some ice cream still attached) is a massive sense of reward/relief (Figure 21). I would like you to keep this concept of 'reward having carried through a successful action' in the forefront of your mind. It is central to learning in the brain.

This simple example of the brain using templates is central to understanding how your brain works as it underpins most of the functionality of your brain. How does this relate to emotional 'health/unhealth'? Well, all your painful memories, your remembered slights, your damaged perceptions of the world, your happiest moments, are all experienced through the activation of templates. All these memories of smells, of tastes, of fear, of happiness are stored in your brain as templates. So the next step towards understanding yourself is to understand how templates are formed in the first place. To do this you need to know about the chemistry that underlies this learning process, and this is what I want to discuss in the next chapter.

A MASSIVE SENSE

OF REWARD

Figure 21

The concept of 'reward having carried through a successful action' is central to learning in the brain.

Chapter 3

now we get down to the nitty-gritty

What a story we have so far. A three-part brain evolved from our earliest ancestors - the birds and the dinosaurs. Yet it all works together like a huge orchestra of 150 billion players all being directed and controlled by the emotional part of your brain, the limbic system. Huge symphonies of millions of nerve cells are playing in sweeping harmonies and wonderful synchrony as your brain processes and analyses and uses all those little bits and pieces of information that it has stored in the form of templates over the years of learning that has made you who you are at this moment in time. And as you walk forward into your future, these templates will be added to and taken from, new templates will be formed and whole new tunes learned - if you give yourself the chance.

But what actually goes on when you learn something? What is happening in your brain that makes a template form, that makes something stick so that you can recall it, whether it be a word, a poem, a tune, a painful experience, the touch of a lover's hand, or just a new way of hitting a tennis ball?

Well, in this chapter I want to tell you all about how learning happens at the most fundamental level, and how

51

the limbic/emotional brain seems to control and direct what you learn and how you learn it.

You have to start with, dare I say it, some basic brain chemistry. Okay, so you hated chemistry at school. I can understand that. I hated chemistry at school. But if you will just bear with me for a short while, I can show you how everything about who you are and what you do is not just the templates you carry in their tens of thousands in your brain, but is the very chemicals that suffuse your brain and which are controlled with a stunningly beautiful precision by your brain, and especially by your emotional/limbic brain. It is these chemicals that are responsible for the connections that grow between your nerve cells to form the templates that are who you are.

So this chapter is about the neurochemistry of the brain. As I find it difficult to count past three (well, I can go 'one, two, three, lots' which seems to do it for me), I hope it will destroy some of the mystique around this sort of science.

All right, lets get started. The first thing I need to tell you a little bit about is not chemicals but the very special connection that two nerve cells make with each other - the synapse. The synapse is one of the most extraordinarily sophisticated things in the body (Figure 22). As I told you earlier it is a tiny, tiny gap between the out–sproutings of two nerve cells. The part of the connection coming from the nerve cell that is sending the signal is on the end of a long signal conduit called an *axon* (Figure 23).

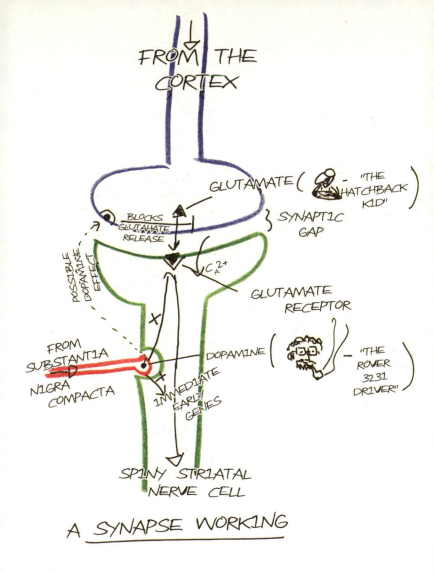

Figure 22

The synapse is one of the most extraordinarily sophisticated things in the body.

The other part of the connection goes to the nerve cell receiving the signal and this conduit is called a *dendrite*. Where these two meet there is a tiny, tiny little gap. Across this gap a galaxy of interactions can occur between the two nerve cells as one sends signals to the other, instructing it what to do, how much of it to do and when to do it.

In this chapter I want to deal with only one of these myriad instructions, and that is the very specialised process of learning. If who you are is because you have formed multiple templates, one for every eventuality, you must have somehow caused those templates to come into being - you must have been able to get nerve cells to form synapses with other nerve cells so that the whole lot can fire together in your symphonic dance of synchrony and harmony. Well, that process of wiring together nerve cells to form templates *is* learning. You 'form up' as a human being because you learn an astounding number of things from the moment you are born until you die. All the information you carry in your brain is because some very specific chemicals have interacted across a synapse, and that interaction has established further synapses between nerve cells to form templates.

And underlying all that learning is chemistry - the astounding chemistry of the brain.

Figure 22 shows a synapse. This is the connection between two nerves. As I have said, the out-sproutings from the two nerves do not actually touch each other but

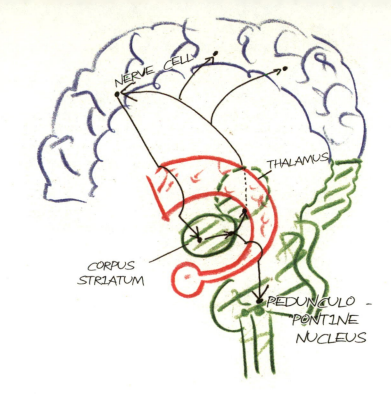

NERVE CELL

THALAMUS

CORPUS STRIATUM

PEDUNCULO - PONTINE NUCLEUS

THE BRAIN IS "POINT-TO-POINT" MAPPED WITH VERY LITTLE LATERAL SPREAD.

Figure 23

The part of the connection coming from the nerve cell that is sending the signal is on the end of a long signal conduit called an *axon*.

have a very small gap between them across which they send chemicals to instruct the other nerve cell what to do. In the diagram, the top part of the synapse is a connection coming down from a nerve cell high in the frontal cortex. It is connecting to a nerve cell in the corpus striatum, and coming in from the side is a connection from a very specialist part of the brain called the *substantia nigra compacta*. This is the structure that tragically in Parkinson's disease stops operating properly. Your substantia nigra compacta is controlled by your limbic/emotional brain and, as we shall see, without its particular chemical no learning of any sort can occur optimally.

The synapse that I am describing is a very specialised synapse and is only found in the corpus striatum (though a variant of it is found in the hippocampus, the other main learning structure in the brain). These two structures, the corpus striatum and the hippocampus, are the only specialised structures in the brain for initiating learning in the rest of your brain. We know that when a person develops damage in these structures they will never remember anything again for as long as they live. I will discuss these structures further as we proceed, but suffice to say at present that your corpus striatum deals with what is called 'habitual' memory (which is predominantly unconscious), whilst your hippocampus deals with what is called 'episodic' memory (which is predominantly conscious, i.e. you can recall it with your conscious mind)[34;35].

The main chemical that operates in this synapse is the first one that I want to introduce you to. It is called *glutamate*. I like to think about things in very simple ways and one of the things I do to get things to stick in my memory is try to give them a human face (Figure 24). Glutamate to me is the 'hatchback kid' of the brain. It drives a standard hatchback that has been souped up to within a whisker of its mechanical ability. It invariably has a huge exhaust (no Freudian analogies please), fat wheels, tinted windows and a stereo system that contravenes the armament rules of the Geneva Convention. The hatchback kid himself is a youth between the ages of 17 and 25, who wears a baseball cap lowered so that it covers the top half of his eyes and who listens to what my 15-year-old son calls 'oonce' music. When played at the sort of volumes that the stereo system in these hatchbacks makes possible, this music is capable of shaking the windows of an entire sleepy suburban street and is undercut by the awesome decibels produced from the 6-inch diameter exhaust. It goes: 'OONCE OONCE OONCE DOOOOM DOOOM OONCE OONCE DOOOM'.

The hatchback kid has two other extraordinary attributes. Firstly he is able to get himself so low in the driving seat that all that can be seen above the side of the driver window is the baseball cap, and secondly he has an extraordinary ability to know a split-second before the traffic light is going to turn green that it is in fact going to turn green. (This particular attribute is one that I have yet to formulate a suitable theory for but there is no doubt in my mind that it is a genuine talent. By the time

A HUMAN FACE

Figure 24

One of the things I do to get things to stick in my memory is try to give them a human face.

the same youth has reached 35 and the wife and kids are in the car with him, the ability has completely atrophied. Curious thing, eh?)

Glutamate is exactly like this hatchback kid. Its only function is to mindlessly excite everything in front of it up to and including the point of death. When glutamate is released from the cortical side of the synapse it travels across the synaptic gap where it connects to a receptor on the connection to the striatal nerve cell. Once it has connected to its receptor it causes the striatal nerve cell to reach progressively higher levels of excitement (this process is called *depolarisation*)[36;37]. What is curious about this is that if this excitation is not halted, the striatal nerve cell eventually dies (Figure 25)[38]. Whilst the thought of dying of too much excitation has a rather interesting (and maybe even appealing) aspect to it, it is not a particularly functional way to get your brain to work over the 75 or so years of your life. After all, if every time you had a thought you killed a few million nerve cells, you would get to maybe have about 300 thoughts and then, whoops, no more brain!

Of course, nature, being a smart old thing, recognised this and another neurochemical is brought into the process. This neurochemical is called *dopamine*. This is the neurochemical which becomes increasingly less available in Parkinson's disease as the substantia nigra compacta gradually atrophies.

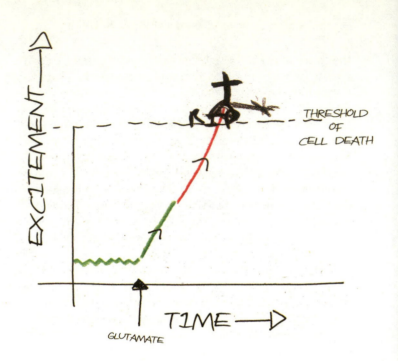

THRESHOLD
OF
CELL DEATH

EXCITEMENT

GLUTAMATE

TIME

UNOPPOSED GLUTAMATE

KILLS NERVE CELLS.

Figure 25
The striatal nerve cell eventually dies.

To get back to my analogy with types of car driver where glutamate drives a souped-up hatchback car. Well, dopamine drives a Rover 323i. A British Racing Green Rover 323i with the natural wood fascia (do I hear you say 'OOOOOOh!'). Dopamine is about 28 years old, male, and wears a tweed flat cap. He would smoke a curly pipe like his father's but isn't yet 30 and therefore doesn't feel he is old enough to ask his father's permission. Wherever you meet this stalwart reactionary he will be driving at exactly three miles an hour less than the prevailing speed limit. In short he is the traffic calmer's dream come true (though he drives the rest of us screaming mad!).

In your brain dopamine acts in a very similar way. It calms down the effects of glutamate.

Now for an extremely important point - dopamine release is predominantly under the control of your emotional/ limbic brain. You must have dopamine release in your brain to learn anything - it is the main synapto-genic chemical in the brain (*synapto* = of synapses, and *genic* = to make or create - so synapto-genic - to create synapses). Learning (the building up of connections between nerve cells to form templates) is therefore largely directed and controlled by your emotional/limbic brain. This is of central importance to understanding learning in any situation. If you have made good emotional connection with the person who is trying to learn from you (or from whom you are trying to learn), you have dramatically increased the chance of them learning that thing from you. It also means that events that have a large emotional content may be learned very effectively, i.e. the synaptic strength of such templates may be high[39]. Of course, having strong synaptic connections does not mean that the event can be readily recalled. It is well known that some of our most traumatic memories are the most difficult to recall.

So what does our nice man in the flat cap, dopamine, do once it has been released. The answer seems to be lots of good things, though not all of them are immediately intuitive. Let me explain. You are trying to learn something. It doesn't matter what - all learning happens by and large in the same way. Let's say you have just got a new car and are trying to work out how to turn on the windscreen wipers (a perennial problem I have with a new car; I spend weeks indicating with my windscreen wipers and trying to clear my screen with the indicators) or you are in school (we can all remember that even if we have now left it!) and the teacher is trying to get you to learn about the history of Iceland.

I want you to imagine that you are interested in what it is you are trying to learn. You are emotionally engaged with learning this new thing (the car I can understand, but Iceland?). Your emotional/limbic brain has got you paying attention to the information (for more on the whole concept of attention see later). Because the higher centres in your cortex are involved (as you are paying attention this goes without saying really) there is already lots of glutamate kicking around the nerve cells in your corpus striatum (and also in your hippocampus). These nerve cells are therefore getting excited. Excellent! Now to grow a template you need some dopamine. Your emotional/limbic brain has been monitoring the whole process and at exactly the right moment releases dopamine onto exactly the right synapses in your brain (how cool is that!)[17;18;40].

So to get back to our original question: what does dopamine do once it is released?

The first thing it probably does is that it leaks out from the synapse with the striatal nerve cell and binds to a receptor on the cortical side of the synapse[41]. This stops further glutamate release - so you will no longer excite your striatal nerve cell to death (a good thing). (It is also worth remembering that glutamate itself also stops release of further glutamate.)

The next thing dopamine does is bind to specific dopamine receptors on the striatal nerve cell. This is just fascinating as the range of effects it produces from this simple act are far-reaching and central to the learning process. The first of these effects is that it supports the up regulation of the glutamate receptor and thus enhances the excitation of the striatal nerve cell[42-44]. The second main effect it has on the striatal nerve cell is on very specialist proteins in the cell called *immediate early genes*[41]. This effect actually keeps the glutamate receptor at a higher level of excitation[45;46].

BUT, but - HOLD ON A SECOND!!!, I hear you say (or think really loudly if you are a silent reader!). I thought the whole point of the exercise was to stop glutamate, the hatchback kid, from killing the striatal nerve cell!

Well, no, I reply. The whole point of the exercise is to start learning whilst *also* preventing glutamate from kill-ing your striatal nerve cell. The actions of dopamine released by your emotional/limbic brain do initially seem counterintuitive as they suggest that dopamine accelerates the excitation process started by glutamate on the striatal nerve cell thus causing its demise. This is not the case. Figure 26 shows an activation curve for the striatal nerve cell. If you look at this it should make sense. Looked at this way it can be seen that glutamate jumpstarts the process of activation (and striatal nerve cells need a fair bit of jumpstarting as they are pretty laid back - imagine the striatal cell is a rural yokel leaning on a fence and chewing on a stalk of grass. Glutamate OONCES past in his hatchback at some ridiculous speed. 'Oooh!! Aarrgh!!' says the rural yokel striatal nerve cell, the grass stalk fall-ing from his mouth and his heart racing with the shock of the glutamate kid's passing). Then along comes slow driving, dead calm dopamine. This arrests the rate of activation at a higher level where it then plateaus (so our rural yokel feels calmer but his heart is still racing). Thus the striatal nerve cell is brought to a higher level of exci-tation that is then sustained[47]. Pretty neat huh! (Figure 26).

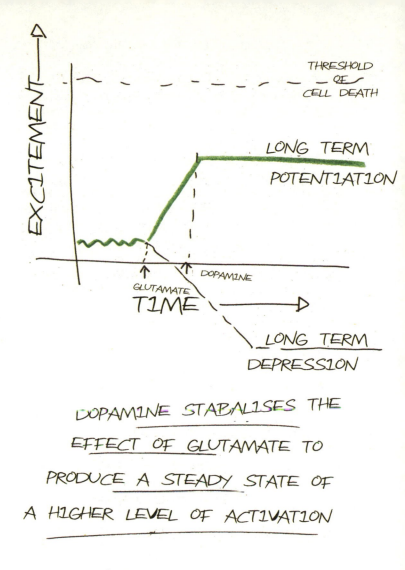

Figure 26

An activation curve for the striatal nerve cell.

And remember, all this is predominantly under the control of the emotional/limbic brain. *Your emotional self is centrally involved in the vast majority of the things you learn.*

Once your striatal nerve cell has got to this higher level of excitation, it can be preserved for minutes, hours or weeks. This in itself is amazing. The normal firing time of a striatal nerve cell is a couple of hundred milliseconds. To have a process on board that allows it to fire for weeks is just extraordinary! (Figure 27). This sustained activation is known as *long term potentiation* and it and its opposite long term depression are the key neurophysiological facts underlying all learning[48;49]. In fact if you cannot start off these processes in your brain you will find learning anything extremely difficult.

It is interesting to note that there are basically only two structures in your brain where the nerve cells are specialised in this way. These structures are your corpus striatum and your hippocampus. They are assisted in these processes by your amygdala (which you remember is one of your most primitive emotional structures) (Figure 28)[5].

Once set up these excitation states are transmitted through the system (Figure 29). One of the fascinating facts about this transmission is the unbelievably accurate way that your brain wires itself together[50-53]. Out of all those 150 billion nerve cells, your long term potentiated striatal nerve cell will only interact with probably a few hundred of them. This beautiful micro circuitry is of

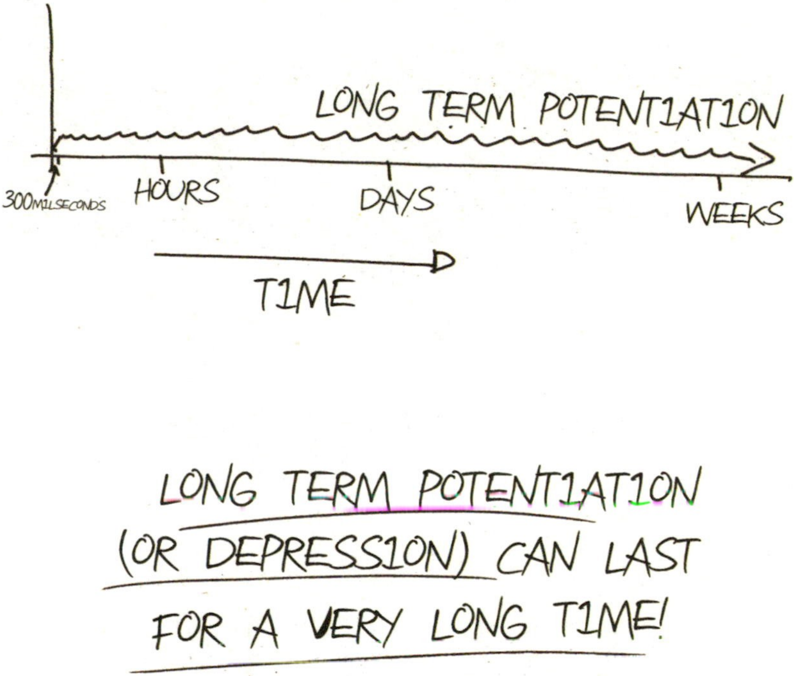

LONG TERM POTENTIATION

HOURS   DAYS   WEEKS

300 MILSECONDS

TIME

LONG TERM POTENTIATION (OR DEPRESSION) CAN LAST FOR A VERY LONG TIME!

Figure 27

To have a process on board that allows it to fire for weeks is just extraordinary!

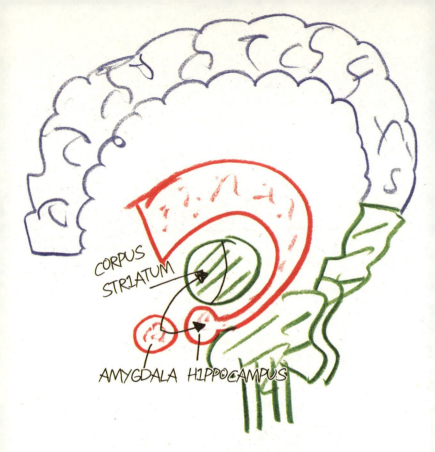

THE CORPUS STRIATUM, HIPPOCAMPUS AND AMYGDALA

Figure 28

The corpus striatum and hippocampus are assisted by your amygdala.

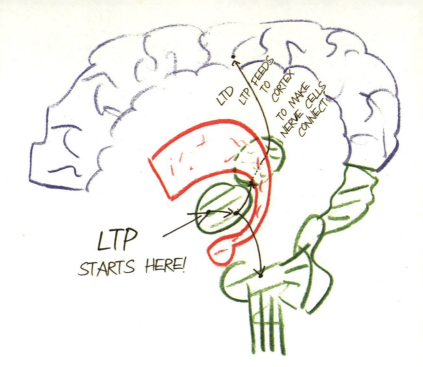

Figure 29

Once set up, excitation states like long term potentiation (LTP) and long term depression (LTD) are transmitted through the system.

course entirely functional. Imagine that you want to move your left little finger (or pinkie, if you happen to be American). It makes sense to 'get ready' other muscles in the hand in case you want to use them as well in whatever you are doing with your pinkie. But it would make no sense at all if you lifted your left leg every time you flexed your pinkie (which of course brings us straight back to Monty Python and the Ministry of Silly Walks. Very, very funny, but not a functional way to get around your life!).

So your brain maps in a strictly 'point-to-point' way in parallel circuits so that areas of function are segregated from each other. Think about the latest *Star Wars* movie and your right arm won't suddenly shoot out into the air (well, there is of course the art of 'air light-sabres' - just the same as air guitar, but infinitely more dangerous!). The loop that your thoughts about *Star Wars* are travelling in is separate to the loop that lifting your arm and performing a light-sabre strike travels in. They are functionally segregated so that the signal from one loop doesn't spill into another loop. Anyway, you get the picture - you only bring on stream functionally relevant areas of your brain for what you are trying to achieve.

So now you are transmitting this higher level of excitation through the system. And what does it do? Yep, you've got it. It stimulates other downstream nerve cells to fire together. And what do nerve cells that fire together do? They wire together. And a new template forms (or you adjust an old template into a slightly different shape)[9;10; 11-16].

And you have learned something new - all under the direction of your emotional/limbic brain, because it controls how, where and when dopamine is released.

For me, this process is one of the most fascinating in our brains, particularly when you place it beside the idea that we are our templates. So whatever you are thinking or doing it is because this extraordinarily elegant piece of neurochemistry and neurophysiology has happened at a time in your past - and you have created the template that you are now using. Even reading and understanding these words means that you are firing off templates that you have learned.

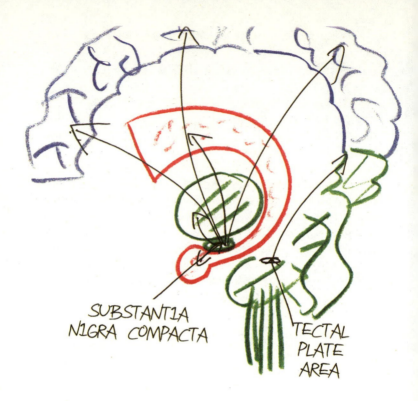

SUBSTANTIA
NIGRA COMPACTA

TECTAL
PLATE
AREA

WHERE DOPAMINE
COMES FROM

Figure 30

Many things can stimulate your emotional brain to release
dopamine throughout the brain.

Chapter 4

making those chemicals dance to a learning tune

So now you know that for learning to happen you need dopamine and glutamate present. And you know that dopamine is controlled predominantly by the limbic/emotional brain. Glutamate is pretty easy to release - virtually anything you do with your nerve cells will release glutamate somewhere in the brain. Dopamine is rather more difficult to release, especially in the very specific way where you want it to hit only the nerve cells or groups of nerve cells that will be involved with learning the particular task that you are trying to set up templates for. Your emotional brain is very sensitive to a large number of things and any one of those things can stimulate it to release dopamine throughout the brain (Figure 30).

So how can you get your brain to release dopamine in the right amount, in the right place and at the right time?

It is important to remember that everything about who you are, how you feel and what you do is because of the templates you have stored in your brain. These templates have become established because dopamine was present in the right amount and in the right places to learn everything from brushing your teeth through simple and complex social encounters to the highest possible forms of complex mathematics. The release of dopamine therefore underpins everything about who you are as an individual.

In fact, if dopamine has been released with glutamate, your brain will learn whatever it is paying attention to at that time - and there is very little you can do about it. So to understand more about why you are who you are, it is important to understand the sort of things that stimulate dopamine release.

The first thing that can stimulate dopamine release is STRESS!!!???>>>:;@!!

Stress is very good at releasing dopamine (Figure 31). There are however a number of problems to releasing dopamine in this way. Firstly: the dopamine released by stress is inclined to arrive in a great flood that bathes huge numbers of nerve cells rather than in the very specific point–to–point way that is ideal for specific template learning. Chronic stress over weeks and months can also theoretically lead to a loss of the ability to release dopamine appropriately. This failure of dopamine release may be the neurochemical burnout that is one possible explanation for conditions such as depression, chronic fatigue syndrome, and a variety of other psycho–emotional conditions.

Secondly: stress produces *adrenaline* and *noradrenaline*. Later on I will talk more about specific memory structures, but suffice to say at this stage that the excess adrenaline and noradrenaline drives memories into the

STRESSED FACE

Figure 31
Stress is very good at releasing dopamine.

Figure 32

Events learned during very high stress situations are unconsciously exerting pressures on conscious life.

unconscious parts of memory. It is certainly possible that because of the high levels of adrenaline and noradrenaline, high levels of stress literally burn memories into the brain and particularly into the unconscious brain. Perhaps in this lies an explanation for post-traumatic stress disorder, somatisation (what Freud called *hysterical conversion syndrome*), and other conditions where events learned during very high stress situations are unconsciously exerting pressures on conscious life (Figure 32)[54].

Thirdly: stress produces *steroids*. Steroids are of course essential for the preservation of life, and some stress is essential for a healthy life. However chronic steroid production has been shown to kill nerve cells especially in the hippocampus but probably also in the amygdala (Figure 33)[55-57]. As the hippocampus is one of the two crucial structures in memory and is particularly involved in conscious short term memory, to destroy nerve cells in it when you are trying to learn does not win as a good survival trait.

So chronic stress is bad for the brain in a number of very fundamental ways. It also has the potential to gradually damage your brain in a way that will make learning more difficult.

So how can you produce dopamine in a way that is physiologically appropriate to normal learning? The two ways of producing dopamine that allow it to be produced in a very specific way (i.e. specifically affecting the nerve cells that you wish to be involved in the specific template

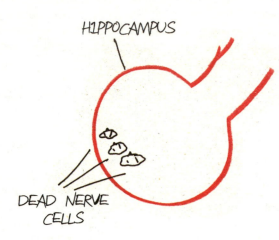

IT WAS STEROIDS WHAT
DID FOR THEM

Figure 33
Chronic steroid production has been shown to kill nerve cells
especially in the hippocampus but probably also in the
amygdala.

to be learned) are through *reward* and the *anticipation of reward* (Figure 34)[18;19;58;59]. This is a huge comment on learning. You are who you are because your genetic nature has interacted with your environmental nurture to lay down templates in your brain. These templates define who you are to the finest detail. Place into that equation the concept of reward and the anticipation of reward. It takes the whole concept of being human to an entirely new level. What is reward to you? How far ahead are you prepared to anticipate reward? How much reward or anticipation of reward did you experience in your childhood?

The mind boggles at the huge number of possibilities such questions raise - and of course the only answers that can make sense are the ones that you generate for your own life. By understanding what rewards you, you start to understand one of the most fundamental things about how you learn now - and how you have been taught in the past. And by *taught* I mean in the broadest possible sense - after all, all of parenting is teaching in the sense I am talking about. Learning is the formation of templates. It is our parents who form some of the most fundamental templates we possess in our brains. And of course not all parents are good teachers even though they may be doing their best. It is perhaps more appropriate to say that not all parents successfully form templates in their children that are appropriate for that child's nature. And here you have the nub of the nature versus nurture debate. I think it is impossible to truly separate out the two in any individual, but it is interesting to speculate

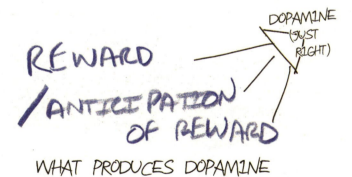

STRESS

DOPAMINE (BUCKETS & BUCKETS)

ADRENALINE
NORADRENALINE

STEROIDS

REWARD
/ANTICIPATION
OF REWARD

DOPAMINE (JUST RIGHT)

WHAT PRODUCES DOPAMINE

Figure 34

The two ways of producing dopamine that allow it to be produced in a very specific way are through reward and the anticipation of reward.

that with sufficient and effective unlearning of templates that are not appropriate to you as an individual, you can get to the quintessential you. Perhaps this is what enlightenment really is - a state of being where your entire brain is harmonic with itself, where no disharmonic templates are present to skew your expression of your true self.

Under conditions of reward and anticipated reward dopamine secretion is firmly under the control of the emotional system[17;18;40] and is applied as though by a painter delivering final touches to a masterpiece.

In parallel to my medical training I have spent 20 years studying the major works aimed at understanding psycho-emotional care. I think it is therefore reasonable to dub myself a humanist therapist ('humanist' = all humans have the right to happiness; 'therapist' = there are a large number of tools that can be used to facilitate any human's journey to that happiness). What has fascinated me most about the process of writing this book is that it is based on working through tens of millions of dollars of research. At the end of this long process (which is still ongoing) the message it has communicated most clearly to me is one that any wise woman in any village could have told you any time in the last 10,000 years. That message? Well let me lay it out for you:

**UNDERSTAND the human in front of you.
Then you will improve their SELF-ESTEEM.**

**If you do this you will improve their
SELF-CONFIDENCE.
And if you do that, they will feel emotionally
ENGAGED with what you are doing.**

(And remember, perhaps most importantly, that the human 'in front of you' is also yourself. Do you understand yourself? Are you good for your self-esteem? Do you improve your self-confidence? Are you emotionally engaged with yourself? If you aren't, perhaps some of those templates that were imprinted on your brain are interfering with you expressing your quintessential self. Perhaps some of the things you have learned are disharmonic with who you actually are.)

This is a very simple algorithm (Figure 35) and can be described in one single four-letter word. I always ask people to guess at this stage what they think that word is. I would ask you to do exactly the same. Take your time. I can wait for as long as you want............................
....
....
....
.... All right. I am sure that you have got it. Just in case there is the odd one of you that hasn't the answer is...**love**.

Selfless love is based on understanding the human in front of you (and by this I mean with your heart working in conjunction with your head, not just your head working alone). This will improve their self-esteem and self-

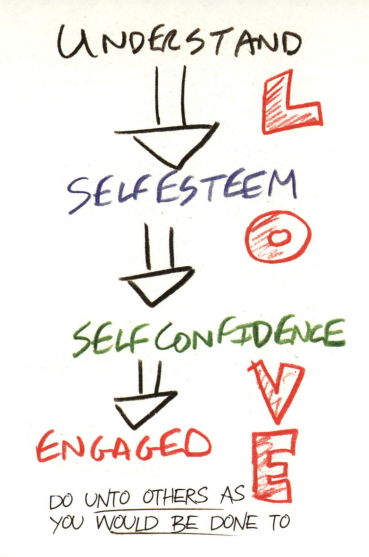

Figure 35

Understanding the human in front of you is a very simple algorithm and can be described in one single four-letter word: love.

confidence. In this environment they will feel emotionally engaged with you and what you are doing. Neurochemically they will have no option but to learn from you. I am sure you all remember one or two individual teachers from your schooldays that you just learned from as if by osmosis. I would suggest to you that the one thing these teachers had for you was the algorithm I have outlined above.

The final comment that I want to make at the end of this chapter is about parenting. I have five children, all of whom I love and am immensely proud of. But learning about how the brain works and the concept of templates and learning have left me with a real problem. I am genuinely terrified of the responsibility that being a parent brings with it. How can I be sure that what I am doing is not laying down templates that will eventually harm my children? The only answer that I have been able to come up with is this: if I do my best to understand my children *as who they are* (not as I might imagine them to be) and I try selflessly to recognise both their strengths and weaknesses now, then I can do my best to encourage their strengths and support their weaknesses. And if I get that right 80 per cent of the time, then that is probably the best I can manage as a human being (and of course wipe their bums, kiss their hurts and just sit and have a good cuddle!).

Chapter 5

the bits that do memory

We have walked a long way together to get to here. You have delved with me into some of the deepest parts of the brain and unravelled their chemistry and their structure. I hope that by this stage it is all building into a shape for you, because it is you I have been talking about. In previous chapters I have looked at the central role of the emotional/limbic brain in your formation. Now I want to look at the actual physical structures in the brain where this amazing neurochemistry does its job to drive the brain to form the templates that are, to a greater or lesser extent, who you are. What you are also going to see again is the very intimate way in which your emotional brain controls and directs memory.

I have mentioned several times specific structures that are the specialised drivers of memory. If I can drop into a football analogy, these structures are the coaches, directing the rest of the team to specific patterns of behaviour and learning (though I hope most of our brains are more pliant (and less expensive) than some footballers seem to be!). The two main structures involved in memory formation are the hippocampus and the corpus striatum. Considering the overall size of your brain (which in an adult human weighs on average 1.5 kg) these structures are very small. They occur in your brain in pairs so there is a right hippocampus and a left hippocampus, a right corpus striatum and a left corpus striatum. The total volume of these structures on one side of your brain is slightly bigger than two thumbs placed side by side running from the top of the thumb to the wrist (Figure 36). That isn't much to base a lifetime of learning on - but in most of us they suffice.

We know quite a lot about what these structures do as, very tragically, it is not unusual for them to be damaged by strokes or injury, particularly in adults. Some of these adults have very courageously allowed themselves to be studied very extensively and this has given us a lot of information. We know that the hippocampus and the corpus striatum have very different memory functions.

Imagine you are sitting with your partner and they ask you how your day has gone. You can relatively easily retrieve this information and starting with the morning you can unroll your day for them so they can share in your experiences. This conscious recall of events that have happened in the very recent past is a function of the hippocampus and is known as *declarative memory* (another way to think about this is as conscious memory, i.e. you can consciously remember the things you store in the hippocampus)[60]. There is evidence now to suggest that the hippocampus is not just involved in very short term memory but contains information relevant to the recalling of events that have happened in the last 15 years or even longer ago[61]. In the tragedy that is dementia it is well recognised that the demented person can often clearly recall the events of their childhood but cannot remember

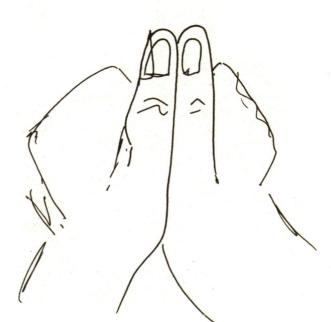

_ TWO THUMBS

Figure 36

The total volume of the corpus striatum and hippocampus on one side of your brain is slightly bigger than two thumbs placed side by side running from the top of the thumb to the wrist.

events from the previous few years. This is because the parts of the brain most heavily affected in early dementia are the temporal and frontal lobes and with them the hippocampi on both sides.

The hippocampus has other functions such as spatial awareness including topographical data[62-64] and I will deal with these in a later chapter when I look at the specialisation of brain areas.

Now I want you to imagine that you are brushing your hair (Figure 37) - in fact why not imitate the action now .... Wait a few minutes and then do it again and repeat this process over the next half hour (if you have nothing else to do with your life!). If you carried out this simple experiment and watched yourself in a mirror while you were doing it or filmed yourself on video you would find that the way your hand moves, the position of your fingers, the position you hold your head in and so on are almost identical each time. This is because you have stored these neuronal patterns in your habitual memory. This is also known as *non-declarative* memory and this memory resides in the corpus striatum (another way to think of this is as unconscious memory or habitual memory, i.e. you use the corpus striatum to store memories to do with your habits of movement, feeling and thinking. These memories are not usually readily available to the conscious mind)[65].

Do you remember from the first chapter that the most primitive part of your brain (the reptilian brain) contains

BRUSHING YOUR
HAIR

Figure 37

The neuronal patterns for brushing your hair are stored in
your habitual memory.

NO MORE PICTURES
PLEASE!

Figure 38

The Mexican green lizards observed by the Californian PhD students were able to perform 27 separate behaviours.

the corpus striatum? The Mexican green lizards observed by the Californian PhD students were able to perform 27 separate behaviours (Figure 38). These behaviours were stored predominantly in the corpus striatum. The corpus striatum in humans has expanded to facilitate habitual memory storage in all aspects of human life. Within your corpus striata there are specialist centres for cognitive, psychological, sensory motor and motor storage where you hold the patterns that dictate the habitual nature of your life (Figure 39).

Both the hippocampus and the corpus striatum are very small structures, which means that they have a relatively small number of nerve cells. Both these structures store templates in their own right. It is interesting to speculate that (particularly in the case of the corpus striatum where your habitual memory resides) the term 'narrow minded' may have a neuro-anatomical correlate in that the presence of very strongly firing templates in the small population of nerve cells available in the corpus striatum may force patterns of feeling and thinking into habitual channels that they find very difficult to leave. If a large number of nerve cells are used up by a small number of powerful templates then the person's ability to be open minded must be dramatically reduced.

Some of you are thinking at this stage, 'Oh my goodness! (or some such word), that means that there is no hope for the bigoted among us!' Actually the opposite is true. For me it is one of the greatest things I have learned from studying the brain. Learning is <u>not</u> just a process of

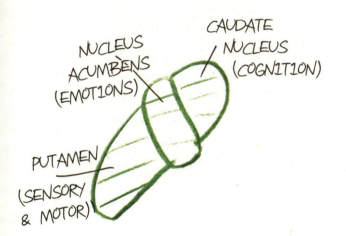

NUCLEUS ACUMBÈNS (EMOTIONS)

CAUDATE NUCLEUS (COGNITION)

PUTAMEN (SENSORY & MOTOR)

ALL THE BITS OF THE CORPUS STRIATUM

Figure 39

Within your corpus striata there are specialist centres for cognitive, psychological, sensory motor and motor storage where you hold the patterns that dictate the habitual nature of your life.

laying down patterns that are then set for all time in your brain. Old patterns *can be changed and be replaced by new ones*[66]. This amazing fact means that you do not have to accept damage that has been done to you - or that you have done to yourself. You can unlearn in a very real sense those templates that are interfering with your ability to lead your life the way you want to. Healing is possible for everyone - though it can take a huge amount of very hard work. This process of making and breaking synapses (and therefore changing template patterns) is called *plasticity*. It is an extraordinary process; dopamine is required for both the making and breaking of synapses. And if dopamine is involved, it means that your emotional self is also intimately involved in the process. In the chapter on the developing brain I will discuss this further.

So your hippocampus deals with conscious memories and your corpus striatum deals with unconscious memories. There is one final memory structure that I want to discuss and that is the most important *facilitator* of memory: your amygdala (Figure 40)[67-70].

The amygdala is your oldest emotional structure - and you have two of them, one in each hemisphere! They reside in close functional proximity to your reptilian brain (though they actually sit in the front part of your hemispheres, the forebrain). In primitive creatures they are responsible for fight or flight reactions, and also for sexual arousal. These functions are still present in your amygdalas. Your amygdala has another amazing function

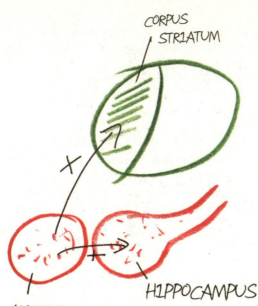

THE AMYGDALA ENHANCES
MEMORY STORAGE/PRODUCTION
IN THE HIPPOCAMPUS AND
CORPUS STRIATUM

Figure 40
The most important *facilitator* of memory is your amygdala.

which is the ability to enhance memory storage. This is an extraordinary ability and it immediately highlights the involvement at all levels of your emotional self in memory.

Your amygdala communicates directly with both your corpus striatum and your hippocampus. Stimulating these connections will increase the ability of these structures to store that particular memory. Your amygdala has receptors for the stress hormone noradrenaline that I mentioned before[71-73]. Noradrenaline can be released by stress directly into your amygdala where it will increase its level of activation. This is then fed in to your hippocampus and your corpus striatum, and events happening at the time of the stress will be turned into templates.

Your amygdala can also be directly stimulated by your *vagus nerve*[69;71;74;75]. Your vagus nerve is the huge nerve that supplies all your viscera - heart, lungs, intestine, kidneys, etc. At times of stress, the stress hormone adrenaline is released into the blood stream. This has a direct excitatory effect on your vagus nerve. This excitation feeds back up your vagus nerve to your brain stem where it further jolts your amygdala into action.

The release of *glucocorticoids* from the adrenals also has a direct effect on the amygdala to increase its level of excitation[76-79]. Glucocorticoids are also known as steroids and are a central part of your body's reaction to stress.

This means that memories learned at times of stress will have significant amygdala enhancement and may therefore be excessively powerful[80;81]. This may be part of the explanation for post-traumatic stress disorder and related psychopathologies. In fact, you can probably recall things now that have happened to you at times of great stress or great emotional arousal. Memories such as these can have a particular intensity to them, a sense of still being just as alive as the day they happened. This is almost certainly because of excessive amygdala drive at the time that you stored those particular templates.

It is also interesting that the more amygdala stimulation that goes into a memory the more likely the memory will be stored in your corpus striatum than in your hippo-campus. Your corpus striatum is concerned with non-declarative or unconscious memories, which means that amygdala activation at the time of storing the memory will make it more likely that that memory will be stored (at least in part) in your unconscious and therefore will be more difficult to access from your conscious mind[54]. This may be part of the explanation for the appalling problems of accessing the traumatic memories that cause such debilitating conditions as post-traumatic stress dis-order in all its forms from the Vietnam veteran reliving the unbelievable terror of being hunted by the Viet Cong to the individual trying to deal with the devastating after-math of being abused as a child.

In education, using terror as a method of teaching was for a long time an accepted practice. Needless to say it is one that I abhor absolutely. The stress produced by teaching through terror may indeed burn the lesson into the pupil's brain but quite apart from the appalling disregard of the pupil's humanity, the pupil will have significant difficulty accessing the information so learned unless the teacher who practised such brutality is standing behind the pupil during examinations with a cattle prod that they are prepared to use.

Once again the point is reinforced that learning should be done in a nurturing and caring environment and not in a situation of systematised brutality.

Your hippocampus and your corpus striatum are absolutely central to learning. Their ability to learn is enhanced by activating your amygdala[5]. But your emotional brain is involved in an even more intimate way within these learning structures. Your hippocampus itself is actually a part of your limbic brain and receives massive inputs from not only the rest of your limbic brain, but also most of the rest of your brain outside your limbic brain. This is a huge convergence of information from both external sources (i.e. outside yourself) and internal sources (i.e. what your heart is doing, what your intestines are doing, etc). It is no wonder then that so many of your memories contain much wider information than the actual facts you may have been learning. Can anyone who has done a number of examinations ever disconnect the smell of fresh cut grass with the feeling of dread of going into another examination? So many important exams are done in May or June - just as the first grass is cut.

Deep in the structure of your corpus striatum are nerve cells that connect directly with your limbic system. These are called *tonically active neurons* (TANs) and they serve to pull together and activate templates in your corpus striatum under the direct control of your limbic/emotional brain[40;51;82-86].

So that just about does it for how memory is activated and facilitated in your brain. How amazing that almost all of how you are formed depends on the intervention of your emotional self. In fact it is probably reasonable to say that the more emotion is removed from learning, the less effectively your brain will learn.

There is also for me an even more important message. It is possible to use this mechanism to unlearn or adapt patterns, to recreate plasticity in your brain. And with that plasticity you can become healthier by unlearning abnormal or damaged templates and reconstructing them in a way that moves you towards increasing emotional health. That for me is such a powerful message. There is nothing about any of you that can't ultimately be changed towards health.

But where does learning happen in your brain? Where do you store all this information on frogs, and walking, and emotional pain, and all those sundry little and large life events that you can recall at a moment's notice? The next thing I want to share with you is the whole concept of brain specialisation, i.e. how your brain divides out all that information. And to do that I will have a look at the whole idea of *brain lateralisation*.

LEFT   RIGHT

INTELLECTUAL   EMOTIONAL

TWO HALVES OF ONE WHOLE

Figure 41

One half of your brain can be considered to be 'emotional' and the other 'creative'.

Chapter 6

why two halves make more than one whole

Your brain is in two halves, and each half contains structures that are twinned with structures in the other half. One half of your brain can be considered to be 'emotional' and the other 'creative' (Figure 41). Obviously there is a great deal of shared function between the two parts of your brain, but there are also a lot of functions that are localised to a specific part of one hemisphere, i.e. that occur predominantly in one hemisphere and not the other. This is called the *lateralisation* of functions. Lateralisation however should be thought of in terms of 'complementary hemispheric specialisation'[87]: even in your visual and auditory cortices where both your hemispheres carry equal functionality, specific items of information are stored preferentially in one side of your brain or the other. Information presented to one of your hemispheres and learned by that hemisphere has been shown not to be available to your other hemisphere when the main connection between your two hemispheres, the *corpus callosum*, is divided[88-90].

This chapter is all about where in your brain you do what you do.

The first thing I want to deal with is which hemisphere is the emotional hemisphere and which hemisphere is the creative and abstract hemisphere. This is an extremely simplistic way of looking at brain functioning as both hemispheres in fact contain both these functions (though with a very different contribution to the overall result). For this discussion however I want you to imagine that one hemisphere dominates the other in terms of these functions.

Believe it or not, the emotional hemisphere is considered to be rigid, didactic, unimaginative, 'in the moment' and driven by very concrete realities (Figure 42). The other hemisphere contains the antithetical abilities, i.e. it is imaginative, abstract, creative, able to produce good rationales for change and is extremely verbal in functioning (Figure 43).

So which hemisphere is which? The answer is that the right hemisphere is the one that is rigid, didactic, unimaginative, in the moment (Figure 44). For a lot of people this is completely counterintuitive as we often equate emotional with creativity. I will try to explain why I think both view points are equally valid.

To put this in another way, your left hemisphere (usually the dominant hemisphere even in left-handed individuals) deals with linguistic, analytic and sequential processing and your right deals with non-verbal, holistic and parallel processing[91;92].

Why your right hemisphere might function in this way is, I believe, best understood in terms of knowing where the

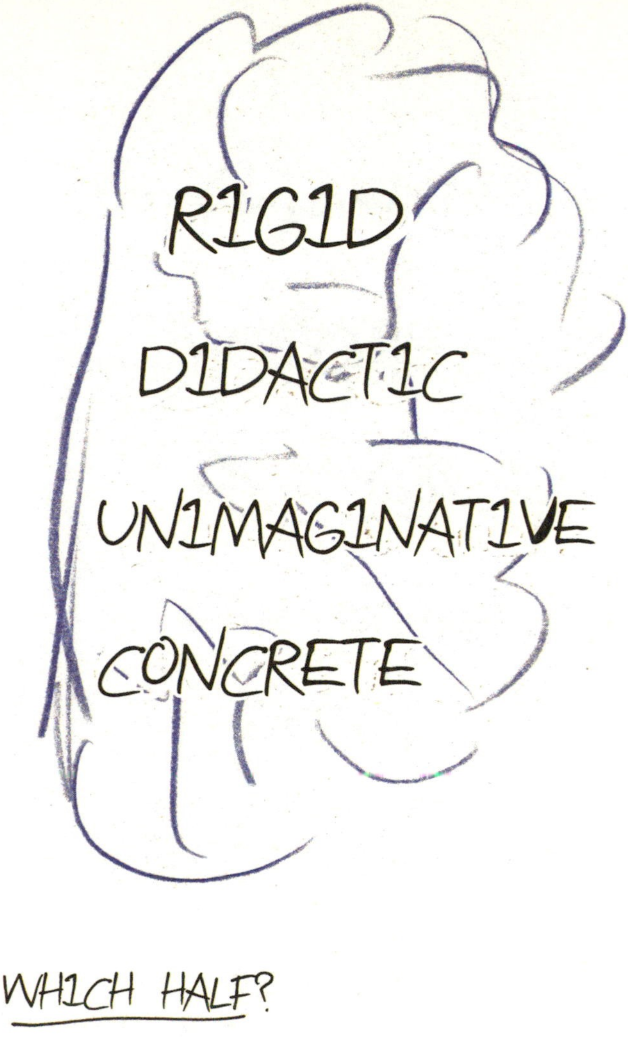

RIGID

DIDACTIC

UNIMAGINATIVE

CONCRETE

WHICH HALF?

Figure 42
The emotional hemisphere is driven by very concrete realities.

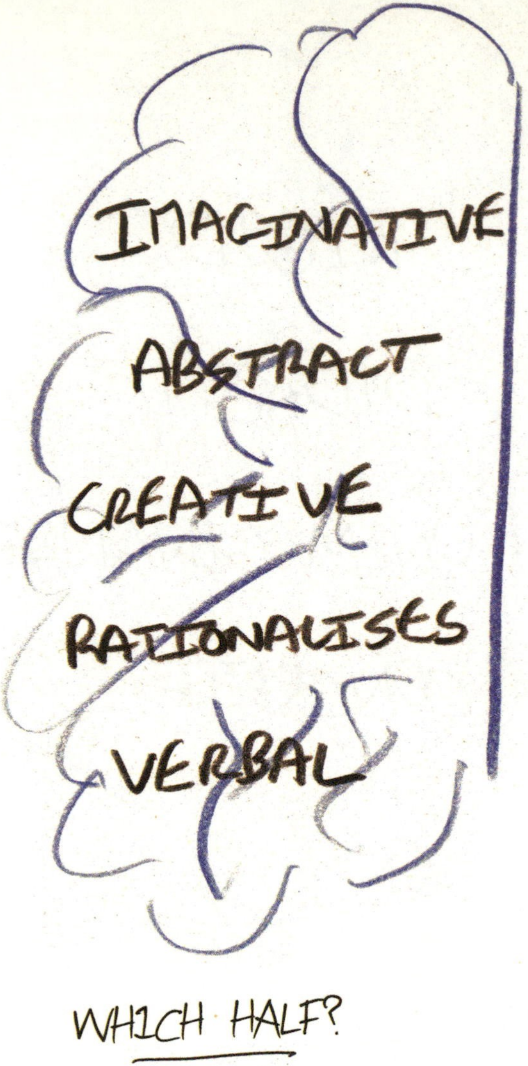

IMAGINATIVE

ABSTRACT

CREATIVE

RATIONALISES

VERBAL

WHICH HALF?

Figure 43
The creative hemisphere is extremely verbal in functioning.

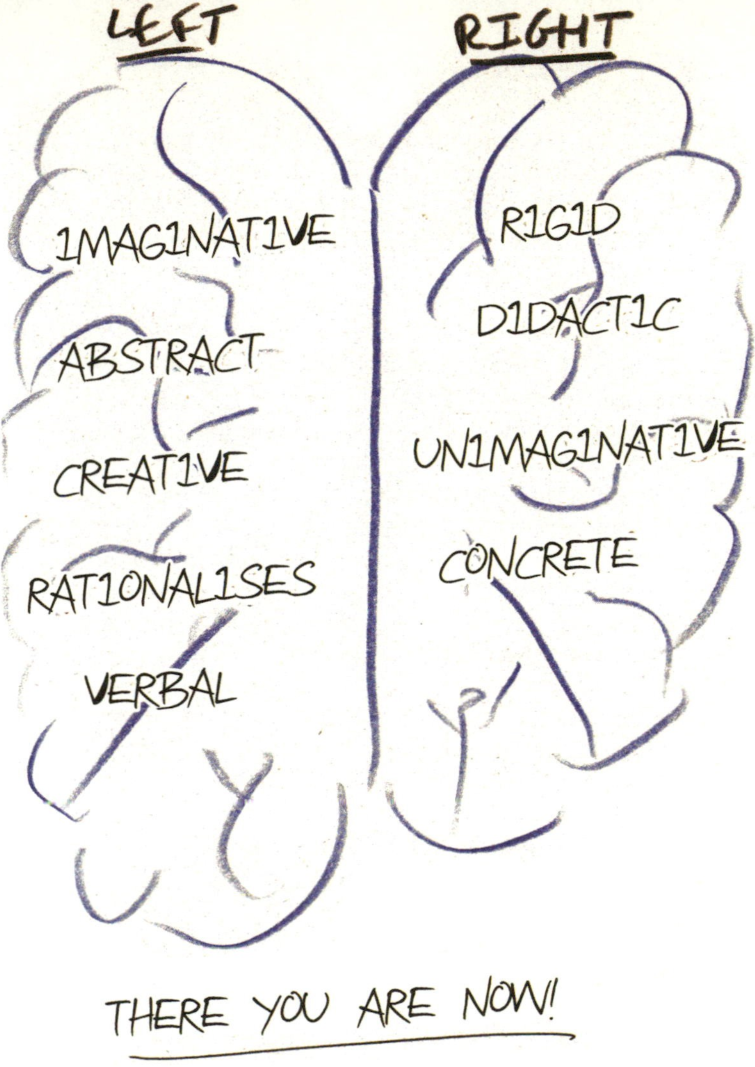

Figure 44
The twinned structures of the brain.

attentional systems in your brain lie[93]. Let me explain. The attentional systems are the systems that enable you to pay attention to both your external environment and your internal environment. Absolutely fascinatingly they are under the control of your limbic system, just like learning and unlearning, and their functioning depends on dopamine[94]. This does make sense if you think it through. If something is worthy of your attention, it is probably also worth learning about - in a purely survival sense most things that are worthy of your attention will either kill you or make you stronger. Learning about both will help you survive longer. Therefore it makes sense to have the two systems of attention and learning both activated by the same structure, i.e. your limbic brain, and as your limbic brain predominantly uses dopamine for its effects, then it also makes sense that both attention and learning use dopamine to function.

By the time you reach adulthood both the anterior and the posterior attentional systems are situated in the right hemisphere in almost everyone (Figure 45)[95]. If (as sometimes tragically happens) an adult has a stroke in the right hemisphere then it is highly likely that they will not be able to pay attention to anything ever again.

It is hypothesised that there are two attentional systems: one at the back of your right hemisphere and one at the front[93]. The one at the back is unconscious in that you are not aware of its work in paying attention to what is going on. It is a busy little body constantly keeping an eye on both your external and your internal environment.

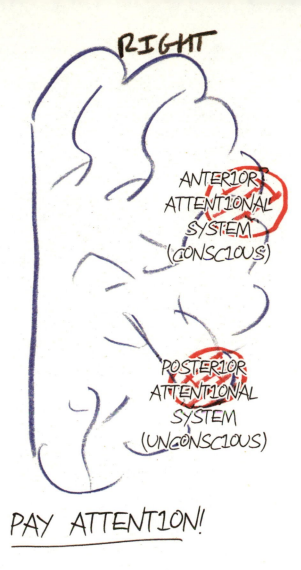

Figure 45

The anterior and the posterior attentional systems are situated in the right hemisphere in almost everyone.

The hypothesis is that it has a set of criteria (in the form of templates) that it constantly compares the with data it is monitoring. Your anterior attentional system is conscious. Once information has reached it, you become consciously aware of what is occurring.

Let me give you an example of how this might work (Figure 46). Imagine you are walking down the street. It is early spring and last night there was a hard frost. Fortunately the council workers have been out and about and have spread salt on the pavement thus clearing it of ice. As is usual you are walking along thinking about the day at work or the nice piece of bacon you had with toast and marmalade for breakfast and your conscious mind is paying very little attention to what is going on around you. Suddenly your foot slips on a patch of ice that has not been cleared by the salt. Your attention is immediately brought to bear on the pavement at your feet as you frantically windmill your arms to preserve your balance. You look down at the pavement, see the ice and say: 'My goodness, that was a close one!' (or perhaps: '!!!!!????@@!!').

So what is the sequence of events in your brain? Well your posterior attentional system on the right was working away monitoring the environment leaving your conscious mind free to think about whatever it wanted. Unfortunately the level of surveillance that your posterior attentional system was using was not sufficient to pick up the patch of ice (and as you know clear ice on a black pavement can be extremely difficult to see). As soon as

SL1PPERY STORY

Figure 46
Imagine you are walking down the street...

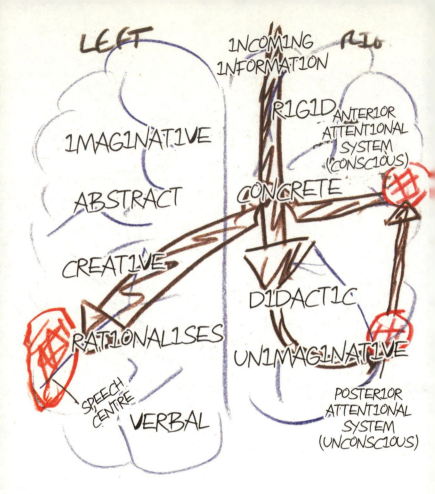

PAYING ATTENTION

Figure 47

Your right anterior attentional system reviews the data
available to it and it streams the information across to the left
hemisphere so that you can give it words.

you started to slip on the ice the unconscious posterior attentional system flicked the data on this threat forward to your conscious attentional system in your right frontal lobe.

Now your right hemisphere contains very little language. Language is mostly dealt with by your left hemisphere. If you want to give words to something to explain it to yourself or someone else, you have to apply your left hemisphere to your feelings or perceptions to give it words (this thought is just fascinating and may be how interpreting emotional pain works. But more on that later!). In the case of slipping on the black ice, once the information had been sent forward to the anterior attentional system in the right hemisphere, you had a strong need to put words to what was going on. Your right anterior attentional system reviews the data available to it and it streams the information across to the left hemisphere so that you can give it words (Figure 47).

Words and most of the other processes of language reside in the left hemisphere in almost everybody (Figure 48)[96]. Even left-handed people (who are inclined to have a dominant right hemisphere) often carry language in their left hemisphere. It is probably for this reason that your left hemisphere is the creative and imaginative one, the interpreter of events[97]. Most of us use language predominantly in our creativity and imagination. Your right hemisphere *is* fully involved in consciousness but it seems to be more in placing your thoughts and ideas in an emotional *context*.

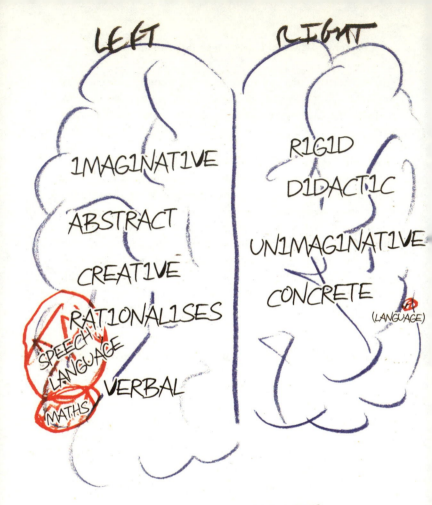

SPEAKING OF HALVES

Figure 48

Words and most of the other processes of language and mathematics reside in the left hemisphere in almost everybody.

Another specialised area in your left hemisphere is that dealing with mathematics (Figure 48). Whilst your right hemisphere is involved in processing mathematical data as well, most of the processing seems to occur in your left hemisphere especially as the sums get more difficult[98]. Even the various aspects of vision and hearing, which are strongly bilaterally represented, may have specific parts of the remembered data that are specialised to one hemisphere or the other.

So lateralisation of function is central to how your brain works. As this book is predominantly written to deal with the underlying neuroscientific information dealing with learning and your emotional self, I don't want to belabour lateralisation much more. To do it full justice would require an entire book all on its own.

I would however like to unpack one or two further thoughts about lateralisation. The first is that to give words to feelings you have to stream information about the feelings across to your left hemisphere where it can be verbalised. There is some work that has shown that stimulating the right hemisphere makes people feel negative feelings, whilst stimulating the left hemisphere makes people feel positive[99;100]. This is just amazing! It also provides a possible explanation about creativity in general. For those of us who are driven to be creative by old emotional pain, it may be that the sequence of events is as follows. A template deep within your limbic brain in your right hemisphere is triggered by something (or it may have such sufficient inherent energy that it can sporadically trigger itself). The feeling it produces is negative, depressing, uncomfortable. In some people the first thing they will do is reach for a computer keyboard or a music–al instrument or a paintbrush or whatever. By then, engaging in activities that bring into play a lot of *left* hemisphere activation, they may feel less negative, less depressed, etc. This is obviously rewarding for them. So they start to establish a behaviour pattern of creativity to counter their underlying right hemisphere negative emotions.

It is also perhaps how therapeutic interventions such as cognitive therapy work. By thinking of something positive to counteract a negative thought, it may be that the brain is not only intellectually creating a positive vibe, but may also be enhancing this positivity by using the left hemisphere to have the positive thought with.

This is pure hypothesis. However I do remember reading a study performed, I think, in Canada where the researchers took 100 creative artists from various genres of art and put them all on antidepressants. Within three months they had all stopped creating. The antidepressants were stopped - and they all started creating again. Now, I am not in any way suggesting that this is conclusive proof, but it is an interesting little study.

A last thought about how specialised areas of the brain might work comes from the researcher Karl Pribram[101]. His theory is called the holographic theory of brain functioning. He hypothesises that a memory is stored across an entire area of specialised cortex. To access that memory any part of that area of cortex can be activated and that part contains the entire memory (Figure 49). The downside is that the smaller the area activated the less detail the memory will contain. I believe that it is certainly possible to support this hypothesis, at least in part, from the images we get from modern functional imaging. When the brain is imaged with these very specialised techniques performing various tasks, it is usual to see most of the area of specialised cortex that is being used 'light up', i.e. become activated. This widespread activation starts to make sense if Pribram's theory is correct - you activate the entire specialist area so that you can withdraw the information you want from its hologram.

Because there is so much shared function between the hemispheres, they have to be able to communicate quickly and efficiently with each other. They do this using a huge bundle of connecting fibres called the corpus callosum (Figure 50). This runs from one hemisphere to the other and connects the entire hemisphere on one side with the entire hemisphere on the other side in a *point to point* way, i.e. nerve cell to nerve cell. Your corpus callosum is another example of the extraordinarily beautiful architecture that your brain displays, this wonderfully detailed mapping of one area of your brain to another so that templates can travel accurately around the system with their information arriving uncorrupted at its target. Nerve cells in a specialist area in your left hemisphere can therefore communicate directly with nerve cells in the same area of specialisation in your right hemisphere by

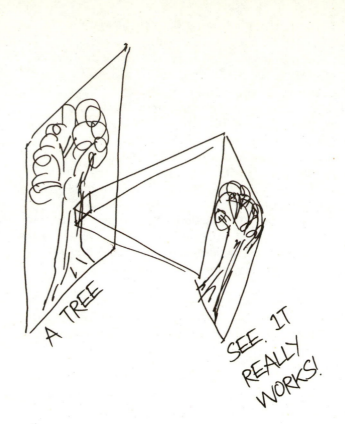

HOLOGRAPHIC THEORY

Figure 49

Karl Pribram's theory about how specialised areas of the brain might work is called the holographic theory of brain functioning.

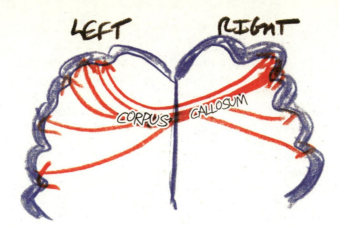

THE CORPUS CALLOSUM

Figure 50

The hemispheres communicate quickly and efficiently with each other using a huge bundle of connecting fibres called the corpus callosum.

the shortest possible route. The speed with which information can travel in your corpus callosum is stunningly fast. It only takes about nine milliseconds for a signal to pass from a nerve cell in one hemisphere to a nerve cell in your other hemisphere when it passes along a fibre in the corpus callosum.

Interestingly, some people are born without a corpus callosum or have had it divided to control epilepsy. It is from work in people like this that we have learned so much about lateralisation in the brain[102].

So finally for this chapter on lateralisation I want to tell you a little about how all this cortical specialisation occurs. I want to make it clear that when I am talking about specialisation it is to an extraordinary level of detail that this specialisation occurs. The micro–architecture of a specialist area of cortex (such as visual or auditory cortices) are very different from each other and from other parts of your brain. As an area of specialist cortex develops it fundamentally changes its architecture to best subserve the functions it specialises in.

How does this happen? Well, the answer seems to lie in the way your brain is mapped in this remarkably accurate topographical way so that your nerve cells form chains of communication and each structure on the chain acts like a relay station[50-53]. A signal arriving from a nerve cell at the beginning of this chain will cause the nerve cells next down the line to move to a higher level of excitation and automatically start to 'burst fire' (Figure 51). Burst firing

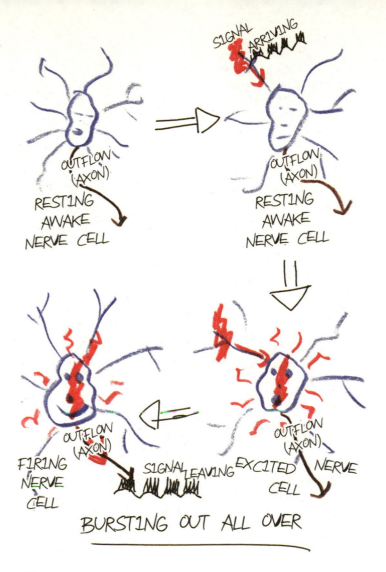

SIGNAL ARRIVING

OUTFLOW
(AXON)

RESTING
AWAKE
NERVE CELL

OUTFLOW
(AXON)

RESTING
AWAKE
NERVE CELL

OUTFLOW
(AXON)

FIRING
NERVE
CELL

SIGNAL LEAVING

EXCITED
CELL

OUTFLOW
(AXON)

NERVE

BURSTING OUT ALL OVER

Figure 51

Nerve cells form chains of communication and each structure
on the chain acts like a relay station.

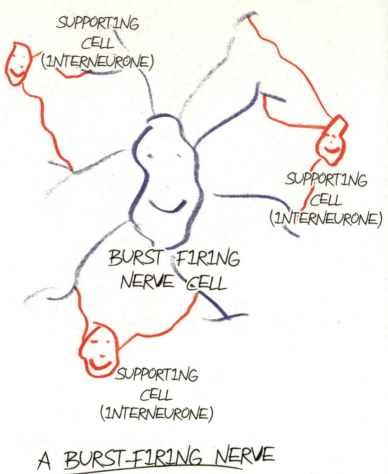

SUPPORTING CELL (1NTERNEURONE)

SUPPORTING CELL (1NTERNEURONE)

BURST FIRING NERVE CELL

SUPPORTING CELL (1NTERNEURONE)

A <u>BURST-FIRING</u> NERVE <u>CELL</u> AND ITS LITTLE HELPERS

Figure 52

Local supporting nerve cells do not have the ability to burst fire.

seems to be the way that your nerve cells communicate with each other[103-106]. It is a very rapid mode of firing that allows the signal to be transmitted at very high frequencies i.e. those in the gamma range (i.e. 20-500 Hz)[11-13;26]. Very interestingly, in each structure in your brain there are nerve cells that act in this burst firing way (and this is a specific ability that they have) and nerve cells that are seen to act in a local supporting way to optimise the performance of these burst firing cells (these local supporting nerve cells do not have the ability to burst fire) (Figure 52).

Deep in your hemispheres lies a structure called the *thalamus* (Figure 53). This is an extremely complicated piece of brain machinery that receives signals from and transmits signals to your entire brain. The two different types of nerve cells that I mentioned above, i.e. burst firing and oscillating, have been studied particularly in the thalamus[107-110]. It is the rhythms produced in your thalamus working together with another structure that sits just beside it, the *reticular nucleus* of the thalamus, which dictates how awake you are.

All the information that reaches your cortex is routed through the thalamus and it is the signal and the nature of the signal coming from your thalamus that seems to create the beautiful micro-architectural changes in your cortex and optimises how your cortex functions in a specialist area. Put another way, if your thalamus transmits visual information to a part of your cortex, then that area

RETICULAR NUCLEUS OF THE THALAMUS

THALAMUS

THE MAIN PACEMAKER

Figure 53

The thalamus receives signals from and transmits signals to the entire brain.

of cortex will gradually change its architecture so that it can function as fully operational visual cortex[111].

The next step on my journey towards understanding global brain functioning is based on how your brain develops from conception through to death. Can one expect a child of 9 to act in all respects like an adult? The answer to that is a resounding no, and I will explain why in the next chapter.

WE ALL DO GET
OLDER!

Figure 54

How old do you need to be before your brain has reached adult levels of maturity?

Chapter 7

growing a brain

Your starter for 10 in this chapter is to answer this simple question - how old do you need to be before your brain has reached adult levels of maturity in terms of its intellectual and emotional functioning? (The usual answer that I get to this is that, in men, never!) (Figure 54). The answer will probably surprise you as it seems that you cannot expect people to consistently act like adults in terms of their brain abilities until they are about 25 years of age. (Of course, this is simply an average figure and many individuals will take shorter or longer to achieve this result.) This has huge implications for your emotional development. It is certainly possible that events that cause emotional damage occurring at different stages of brain development cause different pathologies because they are occurring at these different stages of brain development. i.e. the brain is specifically vulnerable to damage in specific structures at various stages of its growth. To unpack that a little further it is possible that the most severe psychiatric conditions such as schizophrenia and perhaps psychopathic illness are thought in some cases to result from emotional damage occurring before the age of 5 or 6 years of age. The structures damaged in this case would be the deeper, more primitive structures such as the corpus callosum. The obsessive and depressive disorders may relate to damage occurring between 5 and 6 and 10 or 11 (where the structures affected may be

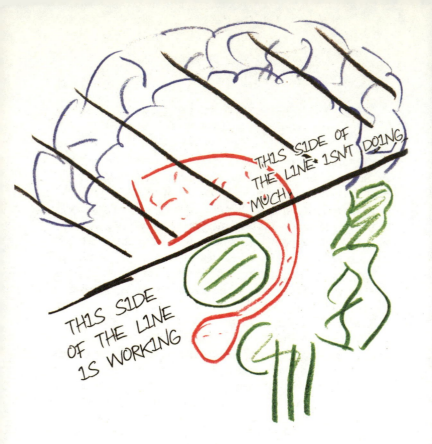

THIS SIDE OF THE LINE ISN'T DOING MUCH.

THIS SIDE OF THE LINE IS WORKING

HOW MUCH WE USE

AS BABIES

Figure 55

The brain stem is part of your reptilian brain and deals with all the basic functions you need to stay alive, such as keeping your heart beating and your lungs breathing.

paleomammalian limbic structures) and the personality disorders and anxiety states may be due to damaging events occurring between 9 and 10 and 14 to 15 (where the structures involved may be in higher cortical areas and their controlling systems). I would reiterate that these are purely hypothetical statements, but may contain some truth.

Why should your brain take 25 years to reach full levels of efficiency and create the stunningly beautiful micro–architecture that the adult human brain contains? Well, your brain is such a wonderfully complex structure that even though you are born with all the nerve cells that you are going to get (which as I have said is probably in the region of 150 billion!) these nerve cells have not yet established the myriad connections that exist within an adult brain. These connections need to mature and develop to create the anatomical changes needed for your brain to function at its full potential (see Chapter 6 on specialisation and lateralisation).

So how does this all start? An extraordinary new discovery in the last 10 years has been that newborn infants function on only a very small part of the brain called the brain stem (if you remember this is part of your reptilian brain and deals with all the basic functions you need to stay alive - things such as keeping your heart beating and your lungs breathing) (Figure 55). Some children are tragically born with no higher brain at all. Even to an experienced neurologist these children can be completely normal on examination until 3 to 4 months of age. It is

CHALK

CLEAN SLATE

WE START OUT WITH
NOTHING WRITTEN

Figure 56

A newborn baby's brain is a clean slate ready to receive new learning.

only after this time that their deficiencies become apparent.

It is also now apparent that a newborn baby's brain is a clean slate ready to receive new learning (Figure 56). Other than a few primitive reflexes that seem to be genetically determined and reside in the brain stem newborn babies have no stored templates.

It is of course fashionable to play classical music to infants still in the womb (Figure 57). Playing classical music to babies is reported to have a relaxing effect on the baby once it is born. I do not personally see this as an example of complex learning in the sense that I have been talking about in this book. I would suggest that what has happened in this instance is that the mother has experienced relaxation from the music. This relaxation has transmitted itself (perhaps through hormonal release in the mother) to the unborn baby. At a basic chemical level the baby learns to associate hearing classical music with this induced relaxation. It seems reasonable to suppose that this conditioned reflex can then still be triggered by classical music once the child is born. Of course, this is still a great thing for the baby! (And not half bad for the parents if they have an easy way of getting their child to sleep.)

Brain development occurs in two main ways. Firstly, the nerve cells in the outer part of your brain, the cortex, have connections with the nerve cells in the middle of your brain (in structures such as your thalamus, your

LISTENING TO THE

VIBE

Figure 57

Playing classical music to infants still in the womb is reported to have a relaxing effect on the baby after it has been born.

basal ganglia, and your brain stem). These connections or 'long tracts' are called *axons*. In the newborn baby they are not yet ready to transmit signals efficiently between these groups of nerve cells. The reason for this is that the axons have not yet been insulated. Imagine that they are like a handful of copper wires in a beaker of salty water. Putting electricity in at one end of a single copper wire will only achieve the spreading out of that electricity through all the other copper wires and the beaker of salty water. The signal will not travel from one end of the copper wire to the other. To get a signal from one end of your copper wire to the other end of the same copper wire you need to insulate the copper wire from its fellows and from the salty water. In your brain a very specialised structural cell forms this insulation. This cell, called a Schwann cell, creates a coat called *myelin* around the connection (Figure 58). The process of gradual insulation of individual connectors in your brain is called *myelination* and it is usually not complete until you are 15 to 17 years of age[112].

Myelination is therefore the first part of brain maturation that needs to occur so that your brain can function efficiently. The second part is the entire process of learning that I have already discussed. The connecting together of your nerve cells through synapses at the local level in your brain over 25 years creates the beautiful galleries and citadels of micro-architecture that can be seen in the brain under the microscope. And in my opinion it is here that trying to differentiate between nature and nurture fundamentally falls apart. The billions and billions of transactions that occur to create the unimaginably

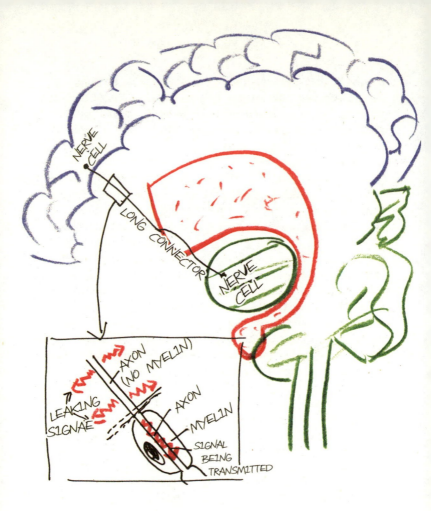

Labels within figure:
NERVE CELL
LONG CONNECTOR
NERVE CELL
AXON (NO MYELIN)
LEAKING SIGNAE
AXON
MYELIN
SIGNAL BEING TRANSMITTED

WRAPPING IT ALL UP

Figure 58

A Schwann cell creates a coat called myelin around the axon in a newborn baby.

complex interconnectedness of nerve cells are the result of the ongoing interaction between your genetic potentials and your environmental experience. Even the esoteric philosophy of chaos mathematics is not yet able to predict in any individual the results of these interactions over their lifetime.

We can however suggest how environments can affect anatomical development. We know from a number of studies, including the tragic plight of orphans left completely alone in cots from shortly after birth[113-115], that abusive and unnurturing environments can cause significant structural abnormalities in the brain. In the example of the ignored orphans their amygdalas were inclined to be small and scarred and they had multiple other anatomical abnormalities throughout their brains. These pathological changes in their brains seem to have been caused entirely by lack of appropriate emotional care. This is an extreme example but it does show how powerfully the environment can affect how your brain develops.

On the other hand, an environment which produces dysharmonic patterns in a human being can appear to be extremely nurturing and loving. I think it is reason-able to suppose that all human beings experience some blunting of their potential in the way that they are parented and interact with their environment as they grow. This is part of the normal human condition. The question, I think, any individual must ask themselves is how much of who you are is who *you* want to be and how much of who you are is how *other people* expect you to be. Of course there may be a large overlap between these two individuals and that can be a very positive thing. After all, to exist in society our behaviours need to fall inside the expected mores.

Which leads me very nicely to the final chapter - how behavioural control works.

Chapter 8

behave or else

This final chapter is about behaviour. By that I mean behaving in a way that allows you to function successfully within your society. A very large part of this is emotional intelligence i.e. the ability to be aware of your own feelings and other people's feelings. This ability is, of course, a large part of emotional health - if you can be aware of things within you that interfere with your health, then you can do something about them. This of course was something that I mentioned in the first chapter - this ability to think about thinking that you contain within your huge neomammalian cortex.

The reason I have left this chapter to the end is because the whole concept of emotional intelligence and how your brain structurally contains and controls behaviours is so central to everything I have talked about. It is this knowledge that can help you heal yourself. It is this wonderful, extraordinary concept that I wanted to be the final word in this song.

The place I always start in thinking about behaviour is our old friend the amygdala, your oldest and most primitive emotional structure, that deep denizen of egocentric, self-survival based behaviours.

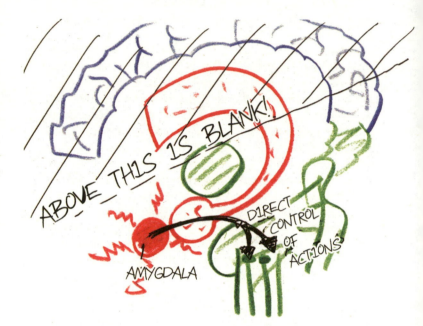

WHAT HAPPENS WHEN THE
AMYGDALA IS AT FULL STOMP

Figure 59

The amygdala has the extraordinary ability to take over basic
motor and emotional functioning in your brain whilst shorting
out higher centres.

One of the extraordinary abilities that your amygdala has is the ability to take over basic motor and emotional functioning in your brain whilst shorting out your higher centres (Figure 59)[116;117]. In survival terms this is pretty sensible. Imagine you are one of your primitive ancestors out for a quiet stroll after dinner (not a very likely picture as dinner was the half cooked rear end of a pig and the only tooth pick you have is a four inch long thorn from a bush). As you perambulate gently down the undulations of the valley in front of your cave, a sabre tooth tiger sticks its head out from behind a bush and makes a grab for your right leg.

At this moment in your life you can do one of two things. You can regard the huge set of canines rushing at your right leg and think, 'My goodness. That looks just like a aaaaaaargh!' as old toothy gets a good grip on your thigh. Or you can already be running at your best approxima-tion of an Olympic athlete's sprinting style back up the hill to your cave before your brain even registers that it *is* a sabre tooth tiger.

It is this second ability that keeps you alive and is central to your amygdala's functions. As it can short out all your higher centres and get you reacting before you can think, you can be out of (and I suppose into) trouble before you even know it's there.

In practical terms shorting out higher centres means removing from your actions all those things associated with higher brain functioning such as conscience,

137

SEE TEXT

Figure 60

The amygdala contains one of the main centres for sexual arousal.

thoughtfulness, planning abilities, etc. It means that an individual being driven entirely by their amygdala would be responding in a mindless and reflexive way to whatever was going on.

The amygdala also contains one of the main centres for sexual arousal (Figure 60). This means that an individual being driven entirely from their amygdala is not only acting mindlessly but is probably getting a massive degree of sexual arousal. If you are unfortunate enough to watch football hooligans or rioters on television it is worthwhile remembering that their main motivation is probably the same as that of a reptile, i.e. it is entirely based around self-gratification with little thought for consequence either to themselves or to other people.

In your brain the amygdala has developed a long way from its primitive forebears and now contains specialist areas for all aspects of higher brain function. This means it is possible to get a fully self-centred influence into all the actions of your brain. Now this is neither a good thing nor a bad thing. It is just who we all are as humans. It can be argued that the more altruistic the action, the more personal reward that individual is getting from their altruism - and there is nothing wrong with a good bit of altruism. It is also commonly said that you need to be responsible for yourself first before you can be responsible for other people (which is really just skinning the same cat from a different end).

Figure 61

For a squirrel, threat probably has claws and sharp teeth and smells dangerous.

Another way of thinking about amygdala function is as an assessor of threat[118-121]. Assessing threat (which is your amygdala's main biological function) becomes an increasingly complex comment the more complex the behaviours of the animal are. For a squirrel, threat probably has claws and sharp teeth and smells dangerous (Figure 61). For you it can be the mildest inflexion on a word when spoken by a rival at work.

For humans therefore threat and what you as an individual *perceive* as threatening can be incredibly complex and very different from one individual to another depending on their life experiences. Your amygdala has areas dealing with most aspects of higher brain functioning. This means, as I have said, that it can insert its egocentric, self-serving influence into most if not all of your brain activities. It is an interesting (and often alarming) exercise to think back over your day and try and divide out the selfishness of what you did from the selflessness of what you did (though don't be too judgmental on yourself.) To preserve our identities as individual human beings we all need to have a good dollop of selfishness mixed in with the selflessness - it's all really just a question of balance.

It has always fascinated me that the human brain has great difficulty in understanding negative commands. 'Don't do that' and 'Don't touch that' and 'Don't!' 'Don't!' 'Don't!' 'DON'T!' What the child *actually* hears is, 'Pick that up' and 'Run' and 'Shout' conveniently dropping the negative from the beginning of the commands (Figure 62).

Figure 62
The human brain has great difficulty in understanding negative commands.

This is just one of the curious ways that your brain works. But how do you gain control of your amygdala? How do you adjust the primitive hedonistic drives from these deep brain structures so that you may turn into a socially adept adult?

Your social learning (like all learning) is based on the development and the maturation of templates. Within society, these templates are dictated by the cultural mores of that subsection of humanity to which you belong. Fascinatingly it is not until a child is 3 to 4 years of age that his or her brain is ready for effective social learning. We all know that 2–year-olds are strong–minded awkward little gits but this is an extremely positive thing (though it doesn't usually seem it when you are parenting one of the little barbarians!). The amygdala's job is to collect data on all the bread and butter survival techniques for life (Figure 63). Certainly two hours watching one of these creatures pouring sand from one container to another again and again and again and again seems a fairly pointless exercise (Figure 64). Next time you watch a child doing this remember that there are probably thousands of ways that sand can move from one container to another. What the child is doing is building up a huge repertoire of templates which allows him or her to perform this task more and more efficiently each time - and knowing how to get things to move from one container to another is a basic requirement of survival for a human.

Figure 63

The amygdala's job is to collect data on all the bread and butter survival techniques for life.

HOW MANY WAYS CAN SAND POUR?

Figure 64

Pouring sand may seem a fairly pointless exercise but the child is building up a repertoire of templates which allows him to perform the task more efficiently.

Behavioural learning occurs in exactly the same way. A child gradually absorbs the expected social behaviours from his or her environment as he or she is exposed to those expectations again and again and again and again. He or she forms them into templates that can then be called upon so that he or she can act appropriately in any given social environment. Acting appropriately brings reward - and that reward reinforces the learning of that template.

Why do we view other cultures as strange or alien? The answer is very simply that they have different templates from you and your brain (at the simple behavioural level) views these as being disharmonic simply because your templates are different. Of course the wonder of having a human brain is that it does have the ability to observe these disharmonic responses from inside your own emotional self and create an open-minded and accepting approach to the differences between cultures (Figure 65). The sad thing is that so many humans cannot rise above their first primitive response to something new or strange.

So where do you store all these behavioural templates? The amygdala is too small and its specialisation is in rapid, thoughtless response. The number and complexity of the templates you need to store to become an effective social adult is huge. The amygdala simply couldn't fit them all in.

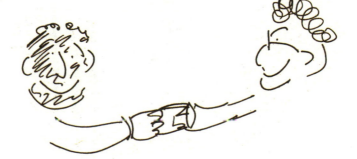

Figure 65

Creating an open-minded and accepting approach to the differences between cultures.

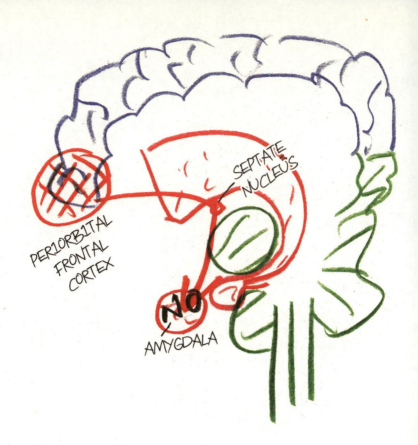

Figure 66

Periorbital means 'around the eyes' and that is where the periorbita frontal cortex is situated.

Which part of your cortex therefore has specialised to perform this task? The answer is the very front of your frontal lobes in an area called the *periorbital frontal cortex* (*periorbital* means 'around the eyes' and that is where it is situated - just above and behind your eyes) (Figure 66)[122;123]. This very specialised part of your cortex carries the templates for your social behaviours - and also for your personality, which of course is intimately connected with your social self. This area has connections to your amygdala - and these connections act to inhibit or calm down your amygdala. So your primitive, mindless basic emotional structure, your amygdala, is tamed by your much more sophisticated, nerve cell-rich higher cortex in your periorbital frontal lobes.

So, what is the time frame for developing emotional control? Well, by about 18 months to two years of life a top-down control system on your amygdala is developing. This starts with your *septate nuclei* (which are a couple of structures deep inside your brain) (Figure 66) and then this specialised area of your frontal lobes comes into play. By the time you are 7 to 8 years of age, this topdown control system should be fully operational.

All our socialising behavioural training is based on this system. From the behavioural strategies of a parent trying to teach a 3-year-old not to stick his tongue out at little old ladies (Figure 67) to the trained behavioural psychologist who is dealing with a 13-year-old with inappropriately sexualised behaviour, the aim is to encourage this top down control of their amygdala.

Figure 67

Trying to teach your 3-year-old not to stick his tongue out at little old ladies.

And this is achieved by, you've guessed it, the gradual build-up of templates that can be consciously brought to bear on the amygdala. So your amygdala sees the last chocolate on the plate (Figure 68): 'I want that,' it thinks selfishly to itself. But Aunt Leticia is ogling it as well. 'I don't care, I want it', thinks your amygdala. 'But wait a minute', says cool-headed frontal lobe and the septate relay. 'You have to offer it to Aunt Leticia first.' SNARL, TEETH GRIND, from Mr Amygdala. But cool head frontal lobe wins the day. Aunt Leticia gets her chocolate. And what happens to you? Well, if you have sensible parents they will have noticed that you didn't snatch the chocolate. On the way home mummy says, 'You did very well not taking that last chocolate and letting Aunt Leticia have it. She is a greedy old thing sometimes.' Big glow of reward in your heart.

And in your brain what that glow of reward means (and the reason you feel it) is dopamine has been released in generous quantities (Figure 69). One of the truly magical things about dopamine release is that it can encourage template formation for behaviours that have occurred a little while ago. So mummy has reactivated all those templates you used to not take the chocolate (I don't know about you but I am getting a bit fed up with that chocolate) - and now she has flooded them pleasantly with dopamine by rewarding you for what you did.

And lo and behold, that pattern of nerve cell firing is reinforced by the dopamine, you grow a few dendrites and flash together a few connectors, and BINGO, that

THE LAST CHOCOLATE

Figure 68

Your amygdala sees the last chocolate on the plate and thinks 'I want that'.

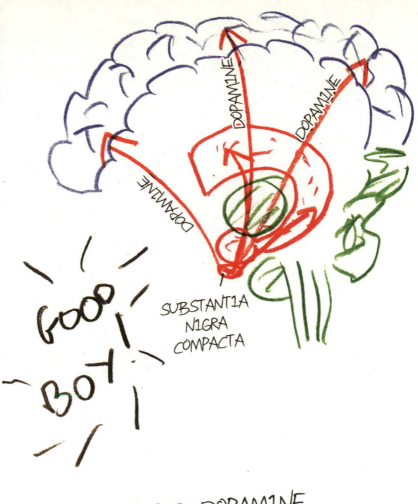

GOOD OLD DOPAMINE

Figure 69

The glow of reward means dopamine has been released in generous quantities.

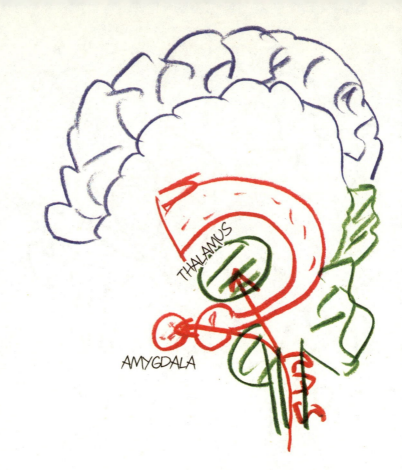

THALAMUS

AMYGDALA

PUMP UP THE VOLUME

Figure 70

The amygdala sits at the top of your reticular activating system.

behaviour has been hard wired a little stronger into your brain.

And that really completes the circle of knowledge for this entire book. You are the interaction between your genetic potentials and the myriad interactions those genetic potentials have with your environments. In your brain this lays down templates under the control of your emotional system. And those templates govern everything about how your brain, and therefore your self, functions. And it all comes down to wiring, the synaptic connections between your nerve cells. Which of course, by appropriate work, can be remodelled to move you towards more complete emotional health.

And finally, no chapter on the behaving brain is complete without one brief and final word about the aroused amygdala (!).

Your amygdala sits at the top of what could romantically be described as your essential life force (which is pretty close to Jung's 'Eros'). The anatomical name for this is the *reticular activating system* (Figure 70)[124;125]. This is an incredibly primitive and powerful system of nerve cells that runs up from your spinal cord through your brain stem to end in your amygdala and your thalamus. Your thalamus (in concert with its neighbouring nucleus, the reticular nucleus of the thalamus) is the main rhythm generating mechanism in your brain (Figure 71)[126]. I hope you remember that the entire functioning of your brain is based on these wonderful harmonic symphonies of

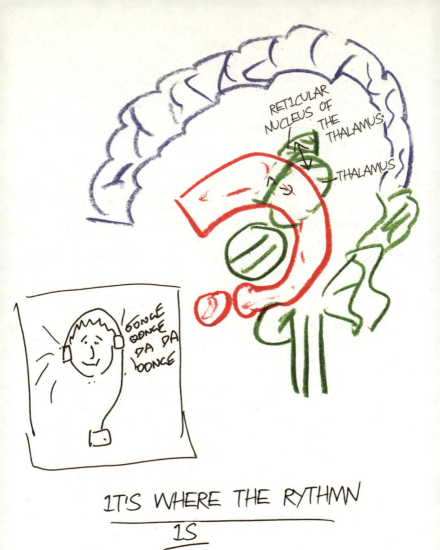

Figure 71

Your thalamus is the main rhythm generating mechanism in your brain.

discharge that sweep through the constellations of connections that festoon your brain. Your thalamus and reticular nucleus of the thalamus are the structures in your brain that make those rhythmic discharges possible.

Your reticular activating system receives inputs from the whole body (Figure 72). Moving and using your body (as well as eating and other things that create changes in your internal environment) provide stimuli to your reticular activating system and this in turn affects the rhythmicity of your brain. The lower the level of arousal in the reticular activating system, the more likely it is that you will fall asleep. Very high levels of arousal produce the opposite effect and if these levels of arousal are high enough they can actually cause your brain to become overloaded with energy and create states of confusion.

Your reticular activating system runs on neurochemicals such as noradrenaline. Your amygdala has actual receptors for noradrenaline and can also be influenced by adrenaline released in the rest of your body. So the more excited you are, the more aroused your reticular activating system is and the higher the level of excitation of your amygdala. In this state there is often very little conscious mind being used (Figure 73)!

So if you want to modify someone's behaviour in a way that they will remember, the first step is to calm them down sufficiently so that their amygdalas are not short-circuiting out their higher brain. This, of course, is the

WHAT TURNS IT ALL ON

Figure 72

Your reticular activating system receives inputs from the whole body.

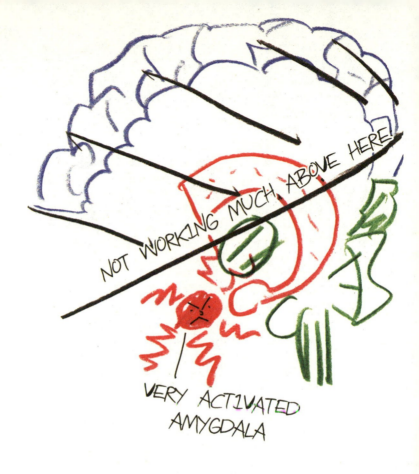

NOT WORKING MUCH ABOVE HERE!

VERY ACTIVATED
AMYGDALA

MUCH AMYGDALA. LITTLE

HIGHER BRAIN

Figure 73
In high levels of excitation there is often very little conscious
mind being used.

neurochemistry underlying behavioural strategies such as 'Stop' or 'Time out' where a child is given time in their own space to calm down.

Once their higher brain is again active, appropriately delivered instruction can then help to lay down templates in the periorbital frontal cortex. And remember, as well, that the amygdala responds to threat. Going toe–to–toe with any individual who has already lost it is only going to wind the situation up further. Back off, take your time and calmly contain the situation. Then you may start to get some results.

Phew! Well, that's it for me. The brain is one of the most extraordinary and wonderful things that I have ever stud-ied. I hope this book has imparted some of that fascin-ation to you - and I hope that having a better under-standing of your brain and how it works helps you on your path. It certainly has on mine. In my own journey so far understanding that it is all down to structure and function has made visible for me my emotional self - and made it clear that there is nothing occult, hidden or sin-ister about our emotional selves. There are as many paths to emotional health and learning as there are human individuals. What yours is is something you can only find out by taking the first step - and then the next step - and so on. But I hope that for you, like me, seeing the prob-lem as ultimately a bunch of wires and connections that need some adjustment will ease your journey somewhat and make it that much less frightening. Good luck!

THE LAST CHOCOLATE!

Reference list

1. MacLean PD. *The Triune Brain in Evolution*. New York: Plenum Press, 1990.

2. MacLean PD. Brain evolution relating to family, play, and the separation call. *Arch Gen. Psychiatry* 1985;42:405-17.

3. MacLean PD. Cerebral evolution and emotional processes: new findings on the striatal complex. *Ann N. Y. Acad Sci* 1972;193:137-49.

4. LeDoux J. Fear and the brain: where have we been, and where are we going? *Biol. Psychiatry* 1998;44:1229-38.

5. LeDoux JE. Emotion circuits in the brain. *Annu.Rev.Neurosci.* 2000;23:155-84.

6. MacLean PD. The Triune brain, emotion and scientific bias. In Schmitt FO, ed. *The Neurosciences. Second Study Program*, pp 336-49. New York: Rockefeller University Press, 1970.

7. MacLean PD. On the origin and progressive evolution of the triune brain. In Armstrong E, Falk D, eds. *Primate Brain Evolution*, pp 291-316. New York: Plenum Press, 1982.

8. MacLean PD. The triune brain in conflict. *Psychother Psychosom* 1977;28:207-20.

9. Skrebitsky VG, Chepkova AN. Hebbian synapses in cortical and hippocampal pathways. *Rev Neurosci* 1998;9:243-64.

10. Merzenich MM, Sameshima K. Cortical plasticity and memory. *Curr Opin Neurobiol.* 1993;3:187-96.

11. Damasio AR. Synchronous activation in multiple cortical regions: a mechanism for recall. *Neuroscience* 1990;2:287-97.

12. Varela FJ. Resonant cell assemblies: a new approach to cognitive function and neuronal synchrony. *Biology Research* 1995;28:81-95.

13. Bressler SL, Coppola R, Nakamura R. Episodic multiregional cortical coherence at multiple frequencies during visual task performance. *Nature* 1993;366:153-6.

14. Vaadia E, et al. Dynamics of neuronal interaction in the monkey cortex in relation to behavioural events. *Nature* 1995;373:515-18.

15. Kreiter AK, Singer W. Stimulus dependent synchronisation of neuronal responses in the visual cortex of the awake macaque monkey. *J Neurosci* 1996;16:2381-96.

16. Rodriguez E, et al. Perceptions shadow: long-distance synchronization of human brain activity. *Nature* 1999;397:430-3.

17. Schultz W, Romo R. Dopamine neurons of the monkey midbrain: contingencies of responses to stimuli eliciting immediate behavioural reactions. *J Neurophysiol* 1990;63:607-24.

18. Mirenowicz J, Schultz W. Importance of unpredictedness for reward responses in primate dopamine neurons. *J Neurophysiol* 1994;72:1024-7.

19. Schultz W. Predictive reward signal of dopamine neurons. *J Neurophysiol* 1998;80:1-27.

20. Kirkwood A, Bear MF. Hebbian synapses in visual cortex. *J Neurosci* 1994;14:1634-45.

21. McClelland JL, Thomas AG, McCandliss BD, Fiez JA. Understanding failures of learning: Hebbian learning, competition for representational space, and some preliminary experimental data. *Prog Brain Res* 1999;121:75-80.

22. Bailey CH, et al. Is heterosynaptic modulation essential for stabilizing Hebbian plasticity and memory? *Nat Rev Neurosci.* 2000;1:11-20.

23. Jo YH, Role LW. Cholinergic modulation of purinergic and GABAergic co-transmission at in vitro hypothalamic synapses. *J Neurophysiol* 2002;88:2501-8.

24. Girod R, Role LW. Long-lasting enhancement of glutamatergic synaptic transmission by acetylcholine contrasts with response adaptation after exposure to low-level nicotine. *J Neurosci* 2001;21:5182-90.

THERE'S MONKEYS BUT NO SQUIRRELS IN THIS ONE!

25. Girod R, Barazangi N, McGehee D, Role LW. Facilitation of glutamatergic neurotransmission by presynaptic nicotinic acetylcholine receptors. *Neuropharmacology* 2000;39:2715–25.

26. Singer W, Gray CM. Visual feature integration and the temporal correlation hypothesis. *Annu Rev Neurosci* 1995;18:555–86.

27. Singer W. Neuronal representations, assemblies and temporal coherence. *Progress in Brain Research* 1993;95:461–74.

28. Nini A, Feingold A, Slovin H, Bergman H. Neurons in the globus pallidus do not show correlated activity in the normal monkey, but phase–locked oscillations appear in the MPTP model of parkinsonism. *J Neurophysiol* 1995;74:1800–5.

29. Goldman–Rakic PS. Regional and cellular fractionation of working memory. *Proc Natl Acad Sci U S A* 1996;93:13473–80.

30. Goldman–Rakic PS. Circuitry of primate prefrontal cortex and regulation of behaviour by representational memory. In Mountcastle VB, Plum F, Geiger SR, eds. *Handbook of Physiology*, pp 373–417. New York: Oxford University Press, 1987.

31. Goldman–Rakic PS. Toward a circuit model of working memory and the guidance of voluntary motor action. In Houk JC, Davis JL, Beiser DG, eds. *Models of Information Processing in the Basal Ganglia*, pp 131–48. Massachusetts: MIT Press, 1995.

32. Picard N, Strick PL. Imaging the premotor areas. *Curr Opin Neurobiol* 2001;11:663–72.

33. Petit L, Courtney SM, Ungerleider LG, Haxby JV. Sustained activity in the medial wall during working memory delays. *J Neurosci* 1998;18:9429 37.

34. Squire LR, Zola SM. Structure and function of declarative and nondeclarative memory systems. *Proc Natl Acad Sci U S A* 1996;93:13515–22.

35. Squire LR, Knowlton B, Musen G. The structure and organization of memory. *Annu Rev Psychol* 1993;44:453–95.

36. Rajadhyaksha A, Barczak A, Macias W, Leveque JC, Lewis SE, Konradi C. L–Type Ca(2+) channels are essential for glutamate–mediated CREB phosphorylation and c–fos gene expression in striatal neurons. *J Neurosci* 1999;19:6348–59.

37. Murphy SN, Miller RJ. Regulation of Ca++ influx into striatal neurons by kainic acid. *J Pharmacol Exp Ther* 1989;249:184–93.

38. Colwell CS, Levine MS. Metabotropic glutamate receptor modulation of excitotoxicity in the neostriatum: role of calcium channels. *Brain Res* 1999;833:234–41.

39. Suri RE, Schultz W. A neural network model with dopamine–like reinforcement signal that learns a spatial delayed response task. *Neuroscience* 1999;91:871–90.

40. Kimura M. Behavioural modulation of sensory responses of primate putamen neurons. *Brain Res* 1992;578:204–14.

41. Onn S–P, West AR, Grace AA. Dopamine–mediated regulation of striatal neuronal and network interactions. *TINS* 2000;23(suppl):S48–S56.

42. Colwell CS, Levine MS. Excitatory synaptic transmission in neostriatal neurons: regulation by cyclic AMP–dependent mechanisms. *J Neurosci* 1995;15:1704–13.

43. Snyder GL, Fienberg AA, Huganir RL, Greengard P. A dopamine/D1 receptor/protein kinase A/dopamine–and cAMP–regulated phosphoprotein (Mr. 32kDA)/protein phosphatase–1 pathway regulates dephosphorylation of the NMDA receptor. *J Neurosci* 1998;18(24):10297–303.

44. Surmeier DJ, et al. Modulation of calcium currents by a D1 dopaminergic protein kinase/phosphatase cascade in rat neostriatal neurons. *Neuron* 1995;14(2):385–97.

45. Lee FJ, et al. Dual regulation of NMDA receptor functions by direct protein–protein interactions with the dopamine D1 receptor. *Cell* 2002;111:219–30.

46. Konradi C, Leveque JC, Hyman SE. Amphetamine and dopamine–induced immediate early gene expression in

striatal neurons depends on postsynaptic NMDA receptors and calcium. *J Neurosci* 1996;16:4231–9.

47. Calabresi P, Centonze D, Bernardi G. Electrophysiology of dopamine in normal and denervated striatal neurons. *Trends Neurosci* 2000;23(Suppl):S57–S63.

48. Bliss TVP, Collingridge GL. A synaptic model of memory – long-term potentiation in the hippocampus. *Nature* 1993;361:31–9.

49. Martinez JL, Jr, Derrick BE. Long-term potentiation and learning. *Annu Rev Psychol* 1996;47:173–203.

50. Flaherty AW, Graybiel AM. Corticostriatal transformations in the primate somatosensory system. Projections from physiologically mapped body part representations. *J Neurophysiol* 1991;66:1249–63.

51. Yeterian EH, Van Hoesen GW. Cortico-striate projections in the rhesus monkey: the organization of certain cortico-caudate connections. *Brain Res* 1978;139:43–63.

52. McGeorge AJ, Faull R. The organization of the projection from the cerebral cortex to the striatum in the rat. *Neuroscience* 1989;29:503–37.

53. Deniau JM, Chevalier G. Functional architecture of the rat substantia nigra pars reticulata: evidence for segregated channels. In Percheron G, McKenzie JS, Feger J, eds. *The basal ganglia IV*, pp 63–70. New York: Plenum Press, 1994.

54. Packard MG, Cahill L. Affective modulation of multiple memory systems. *Curr Opin Neurobiol.* 2001;11:752–6.

55. Joseph R. Traumatic amnesia, repression, and hippocampus injury due to emotional stress, corticosteroids and enkephalins. *Child Psychiatry Hum Dev* 1998;29:169–85.

56. Sapolsky RM, Uno H, Rebert CS, Finch CE. Hippocampal damage associated with prolonged glucocorticoid exposure in primates. *J Neurosci* 1990;10:2897–902.

57. Lee AL, Ogle WO, Sapolsky RM. Stress and depression: possible links to neuron death in the hippocampus. *Bipolar Disord* 2002;4:117–28.

58. Schultz W, et al. Reward–related signals carried by dopamine neurons. In Houk JC, Davis JL, Beiser DG, eds. Μοδελσ οφ ινφορματιον προχεσσινγ ιν τηε βασαλ γανγλια, pp 233–48. Χαμβριδγε: MIT Πρεσσ, 1995.

59. Schultz W. The reward signal of midbrain dopamine neurons. *News Physiol Sci* 1999;14:249–55.

60. Eichenbaum H. The hippocampus and declarative memory: cognitive mechanisms and neural codes. *Behav Brain Res* 2001;127:199–207.

61. Ryan L, et al. Hippocampal complex and retrieval of recent and very remote autobiographical memories: evidence from functional magnetic resonance imaging in neurologically intact people. *Hippocampus* 2001;11:707–14.

62. Gasbarri A, et al. Spatial memory impairment induced by lesion of the mesohippocampal dopaminergic system in the rat. *Neuroscience* 1996;74:1037–44.

63. Best PJ, White AM, Minai A. Spatial processing in the brain: the activity of hippocampal place cells. *Annu Rev Neurosci* 2001;24:459–86.

64. Ikonen S, et al. Cholinergic system regulation of spatial representation by the hippocampus. *Hippocampus* 2002;12:386–97.

65. Squire LR. Memory systems. *C R Acad Sci III* 1998;321:153–6.

66. Centonze D, Siracusano A, Calabresi P, Bernardi G. Removing pathogenic memories: a neurobiology of psychotherapy. *Mol Neurobiol.* 2005;32:123–32.

67. Cahill L, McGaugh JL. The neurobiology of memory for emotional events: adrenergic activation and the amygdala. *Proc West Pharmacol Soc* 1996;39:81–4.

68. Brioni JD, Nagahara AH, McGaugh JL. Involvement of the amygdala GABAergic system in the modulation of memory storage. *Brain Res* 1989;487:105–12.

69. Cahill L. Neurobiological mechanisms of emotionally influenced, long-term memory. *Prog Brain Res* 2000;126:29–37.

70. Ferry B, Roozendaal B, McGaugh JL. Basolateral amygdala noradrenergic influences on memory storage are mediated by an interaction between beta- and alpha1-adrenoceptors. *J Neurosci* 1999;19:5119–23.

71. van Stegeren AH, et al. Memory for emotional events: differential effects of centrally versus peripherally acting beta-blocking agents. *Psychopharmacology (Berl)* 1998;138:305–10.

72. Cahill L, Prins B, Weber M, McGaugh JL. Beta-adrenergic activation and memory for emotional events. *Nature* 1994;371:702–4.

73. McGaugh JL, Cahill L, Roozendaal B. Involvement of the amygdala in memory storage: interaction with other brain systems. *Proc Natl Acad Sci U S A* 1996;93:13508–14.

74. Packard M, Williams C, Cahill L, McGaugh JL. The anatomy of a memory modulatory system: from periphery to brain. In Speer NE, Speer LP, Woodruff ML, eds. *Neurobehavioural Plasticity: Learning, Development, and Response to Brain Insults*, Hillsdale, NJ: Lawrence Erlbaum Associates, 1995.

75. Clark KB, et al. Enhanced recognition memory following vagus nerve stimulation in human subjects. *Nat Neurosci* 1999;2:94–8.

76. Roozendaal B, et al. Involvement of stress–released corticotropin–releasing hormone in the basolateral amygdala in regulating memory consolidation. *Proc Natl Acad Sci U S A* 2002;99:13908–13.

77. Roozendaal B, Quirarte GL, McGaugh JL. Glucocorticoids interact with the basolateral amygdala beta-adrenoceptor –cAMP/cAMP/PKA system in influencing memory consolidation. *Eur J Neurosci* 2002;15:553–60.

78. Roozendaal B. 1999 Curt P. Richter award. Glucocorticoids and the regulation of memory consolidation. *Psychoneuro-endocrinology* 2000;25:213–38.

79. Quirarte GL, Roozendaal B, McGaugh JL. Glucocorticoid enhancement of memory storage involves noradrenergic activation in the basolateral amygdala. *Proc Natl Acad Sci U S A* 1997;94:14048–53.

80. Kesner RP, Wilburn MW. A review of electrical stimulation of the brain in context of learning and retention. *Behav Biol* 1974;10:259–93.

81. McGaugh JL, Gold PE. In Rosenzweig MR, Bennett EL, eds. *Neural Mechanisms of Learning and Memory*, pp 549–60. Cambridge, MA: MIT Press, 1976.

82. Graybiel AM, Aosaki T, Flaherty A, Kimura M. The basal ganglia and adaptive motor control. *Science* 1994;265:1826–31.

83. Aosaki T, et al. Responses of tonically active neurons in the primates striatum undergo systematic changes during behavioural sensorimotor conditioning. *J Neurosci* 1994;14(6):3969–84.

84. Graybiel AM. The basal ganglia and chunking of action repertories. *Neurobiology of Learning and Memory* 1998;70:119–36.

85. Flaherty A, Graybiel A. Corticostriatal transformation in the primate somatosensory system. Projections from physiologically mapped body–part representations. *J Neurophysiol* 1991;66:1249.

86. Graybiel AM. Building action repertories: memory and learning functions of the basal ganglia. *Current Opinion in Neurobiology* 1995;5:733–41.

87. Heilman KM, Gilmore RL. Cortical influences in emotion. *J Clin Neurophysiol* 1998;15:409–23.

88. Corballis PM, Funnell MG, Gazzaniga MS. Hemispheric asymmetries for simple visual judgments in the split brain. *Neuropsychologia* 2002;40:401–10.

89. Spence C, Kingstone A, Shore DI, Gazzaniga MS. Representation of visuotactile space in the split brain. *Psychol Sci* 2001;12:90–3.

90. Gazzaniga MS. The split brain revisited. *Sci. Am* 1998;279:50–5.

91. Benowitz LI, et al. Hemispheric specialization in nonverbal communication. *Cortex* 1983;19:5–11.

92. Berlucchi G, Aglioti S, Tassinari G. Rightward attentional bias and left hemisphere dominance in a cue-target light detection task in a callosotomy patient. *Neuropsychologia* 1997;35:941–52.

93. Posner MI, Petersen SE. The attention system of the human brain. *Annu Rev Neurosci* 1990;13:25–42.

94. Nieoullon A. Dopamine and the regulation of cognition and attention. *Prog Neurobiol* 2002;67:53–83.

95. Coull JT. Neural correlates of attention and arousal: insights from electrophysiology, functional neuroimaging and psycho-pharmacology. *Prog Neurobiol* 1998;55:343–61.

96. Zaidel E. Brain Asymmetry. *International Encyclopedia of the Social & Behavioural Sciences*, Elsevier Science 2001.

97. Gazzaniga MS. Cerebral specialization and interhemispheric communication: does the corpus callosum enable the human condition? *Brain* 2000;123(Pt 7).1293–326.

98. Kong J, et al. The neural substrate of arithmetic operations and procedure complexity. *Brain Res Cogn Brain Res* 2005;22:397–405.

99. Morris JS, et al. A differential neural response in the human amygdala to fearful and happy facial expressions. *Nature* 1996;383:812–5.

100. Imaizumi S, et al. Vocal identification of speaker and emotion activates different brain regions. *Neuroreport* 1997;8:2809–12.

101. Pribram KH. *Brain and Perception: Holonomy and Structure in Figural Processing*. New Jersey: Lawrence Erlbaum Associates, 1991.

102. Lamm O, Gordon HW. Right hemisphere superiority in processing new symbols for arithmetic operators. *Acta Psychol (Amst)* 1984;57:29–45.

103. Bialek W, Zee A. Coding and computation with neural spike trains. *J Stat Phys* 1990;59:103–15.

104. Borst A, Theunissen FE. Information theory and neural coding. *Nat Neurosci* 1999;2:947–57.

105. deCharms RC, Zador A. Neural representation and the cortical code. *Annu Rev Neurosci* 2000;23:613–47.

106. Lisman JE. Bursts as a unit of neural information: making unreliable synapses reliable. *Trends Neurosci* 1997;20:38–43.

107. Jones EG. The thalamic matrix and thalamocortical synchrony. *Trends Neurosci* 2001;24:595–601.

108. Lumer ED, Edelman GM, Tononi G. Neural dynamics in a model of the thalamocortical system. I. Layers, loops and the emergence of fast synchronous rhythms. *Cereb Cortex* 1997;7:207–27.

109. Tononi G, Sporns O, Edelman GM. Reentry and the problem of integrating multiple cortical areas: simulation of dynamic integration in the visual system. *Cereb.Cortex* 1992;2:310–35.

110. Van der Werf YD, Witter MP, Groenewegen HJ. The intralaminar and midline nuclei of the thalamus. Anatomical and functional evidence for participation in processes of arousal and awareness. *Brain Res Brain Res Rev.* 2002;39:107–40.

111. Rubenstein JL. Intrinsic and extrinsic control of cortical development. *Novartis Found Symp.* 2000;228:67–75.

112. Paus T, et al. Structural maturation of neural pathways in children and adolescents: in vivo study. *Science* 1999;283:1908–11.

113. Eluvathingal TJ, et al. Abnormal brain connectivity in children after early severe socioemotional deprivation: a diffusion tensor imaging study. *Pediatrics* 2006;117:2093-100.

114. Rutter M, O'Connor TG. Are there biological programming effects for psychological development? Findings from a study of Romanian adoptees. *Dev Psychol* 2004;40:81-94.

115. Chugani HT, et al. Local brain functional activity following early deprivation: a study of postinstitutionalized Romanian orphans. *Neuroimage.* 2001;14:1290-301.

116. LeDoux J. Sensory systems and emotion: a model of affective processing. *Integrative Psychiatry* 1986;4:237-48.

117. LeDoux J. Emotion and the limbic system concept. *Concepts in Neuroscience* 1992;2.

118. Eippert F, et al. Regulation of emotional responses elicited by threat-related stimuli. *Hum Brain Mapp.* 2007;28:409-23.

119. Larson CL, et al. Fear is fast in phobic individuals: amygdala activation in response to fear-relevant stimuli. *Biol Psychiatry* 2006;60:410-7.

120. Suslow T, et al. Amygdala activation during masked presentation of emotional faces predicts conscious detection of threat-related faces. *Brain Cogn* 2006;61:243-8.

121. Vuilleumier P. How brains beware: neural mechanisms of emotional attention. *Trends Cogn Sci* 2005;9:585-94.

122. Dolan RJ. The human amygdala and orbital prefrontal cortex in behavioural regulation. *Philos Trans R Soc Lond B Biol Sci.* 2007;362:787-99.

123. Shima K, Isoda M, Mushiake H, Tanji J. Categorization of behavioural sequences in the prefrontal cortex. *Nature* 2007;445:315-18.

124. Vincent SR. The ascending reticular activating system – from aminergic neurons to nitric oxide. *J Chem Neuroanat* 2000;18:23-30.

125. Garcia-Rill E. Disorders of the reticular activating system. *Med Hypotheses* 1997;49:379-87.

126. Steriade M. Corticothalamic resonance, states of vigilance and mentation. *Neuroscience* 2000;101:243–76.

Index

More Little Books ...

The Little Book of Thunks®: 260 questions to make your brain go ouch! by Ian Gilbert ISBN: 9781845900625

The Little Book of Music for the Classroom: Using Music to Improve Memory, Motivation, Learning and Creativity by Nina Jackson edited by Ian Gilbert ISBN: 9781845900915

The Little Book of Inspirational Teaching Activities: Bringing NLP into the Classroom by David Hodgson edited by Ian Gilbert ISBN: 9781845901363

The Little Book of Values: Educating children to become thinking, responsible and caring citizens by Julie Duckworth edited by Ian Gilbert ISBN: 9781845901356

The Little Book of Charisma: Applying the Art and Science by David Hodgson edited by Ian Gilbert ISBN: 9781845902933

The Little Book of Bereavement for Schools by Ian Gilbert with William, Olivia and Phoebe Gilbert ISBN: 9781845904647

Little Owl's Book of Thinking: An Introduction to Thinking Skills by Ian Gilbert ISBN: 9781904424352

Dancing About Architecture: A Little Book of Creativity by Phil Beadle edited by Ian Gilbert ISBN: 9781845907259

The Perfect (Ofsted) Lesson by Jackie Beere edited by Ian Gilbert ISBN: 9781845904609